Building Student
Literacy Through

Sustained
Silent
Reading

Steve Gardiner

Association for Supervision and Curr
Alexandria, Virginia

D1367846

Association for Supervision and Curriculum Development
1703 N. Beauregard St. • Alexandria, VA 22311-1714 USA
Phone: 800-933-2723 or 703-578-9600 • Fax: 703-575-5400
Web site: www.ascd.org • E-mail: member@ascd.org
Author guidelines: www.ascd.org/write

Gene R. Carter, *Executive Director;* Nancy Modrak, *Director of Publishing;* Julie Houtz, *Director of Book Editing & Production;* Deborah Siegel and Tim Sniffin, *Project Managers;* Greer Beeken, *Graphic Designer;* Valerie Younkin, *Desktop Publishing Specialist;* Vivian Coss, *Production Specialist*

All Web links in this book are correct as of the publication date below but may have become inactive or otherwise modified since that time. If you notice a deactivated or changed link, please e-mail books@ascd.org with the words "Link Update" in the subject line. In your message, please specify the Web link, the book title, and the page number on which the link appears.

Paperback ISBN: 1-4166-0226-7 • ASCD product #105027 • s10/05

e-books: retail PDF ISBN: 1-4166-0335-2 • netLibrary ISBN: 1-4166-0333-6 • ebrary ISBN: 1-4166-0334-4

Quantity discounts for the paperback book: 10–49 copies, 10%; 50+ copies, 15%; for 500 or more copies, call 800-933-2723, ext. 5634, or 703-575-5634. For desk copies: member@ascd.org

Library of Congress Cataloging-in-Publication Data
Gardiner, Steve.
  Building student literacy through sustained silent reading / Steve Gardiner.
     p. cm.
  Includes bibliographical references and index.
  ISBN 1-4166-0226-7 (alk. paper)
  1. Silent reading—United States. 2. Language arts—United States. I. Title.
  LB1050.55.G37 2005
  428.4'071—dc22
                                                              2005019541

12 11 10 09 08 07 06 05   12 11 10 9 8 7 6 5 4 3 2 1

○　　　○　　　○

To the more than 3,000 students
who have shared sustained silent reading
with me in my classroom.

Thank you.

Finding the Words

She had never said a word
in her life.
She had never known what it was like to
create a sentence with her voice.
Until one day,
she reached out
with her hand
and grabbed a sentence
as it floated by her.
She took the sentence by its last word
and placed it lightly on her lips.
She sat with her eyes closed,
hoping that if she didn't look,
the sentence wouldn't be shy like all the others
and run away.
She exhaled slowly,
passing the air over the words on her lips.
"I love you."
She sighed with wonder.
Imagine that, all this time, she'd known how to do it,
she was just starting with the wrong words.

Rosa Carson
Junior at Jackson Hole High School
Jackson, Wyoming
1993

Building Student
Literacy Through

Sustained
Silent
Reading

Acknowledgments

The biggest thanks go to the many students who have spent time involved in sustained silent reading in my classroom over the years. This book is dedicated to them; through their compliments, complaints, observations, and actions, they have shown me what they need as they progress toward becoming Good Adult Readers.

I also want to thank Scott Anderson, Lyn McKinney, Jan Allen, Nan Jones, Terra Beth Jochems, Koby Murray, Kris Keup, and Judy Barnes—all faculty members at Billings Senior High School—for many lengthy discussions about sustained silent reading and for the encouragement to collect the essence of those conversations here.

Thank you to Judy Barnes, Kris Keup, and Vince Long for reading the manuscript and giving freely of their comments. Also, an extra thanks to Vince for his help with a long list of technology issues, especially online publishing, and for his support and enthusiasm as we pursued master's degrees, National Board Certification, marathon running, and a thousand interesting lunch topics together.

Thank you to Scott Willis and the staff at ASCD, who believed in this project from the first time they heard about it, and to Tim Sniffin, whose careful and caring editorial eye made this a better book.

Finally, to my girls, Peggy, Greta, Romney, and Denby, my love.

Preface

I didn't like high school English. Everything we read was chosen by the teacher. We read at a rate assigned by the teacher, discussed the parts selected by the teacher, and answered questions the way we thought the teacher wanted them answered. Consequently, I didn't enjoy reading and seldom finished assigned books, except one.

It was 1969 and the teacher let us choose any book we wanted to read. Advertisements for Mario Puzo's *The Godfather* bombarded me, so I chose that. Caught by the excitement and suspense, I read every single page, gave my book report, and scored the highest grade I had ever received in English class. I felt good.

The teacher, far too progressive for a rural midwestern town, resigned after his first year. I, along with other students, returned to teachers who assigned every book for the year. They were good books: Hawthorne, Melville, Thoreau, Emerson, Shakespeare—core curriculum in many school districts—but not the books I wanted to read. I simply wasn't ready for those books, so I didn't read them.

In college as a math major, I determined to avoid unnecessary exposure to English teachers, which was easy until an injury forced me to spend a week in bed. A friend visited and brought a couple of paperback novels. I accepted them (I couldn't be rude), but later tossed them on a shelf with a chuckle.

Later, the chuckle turned to boredom; I picked up one of the books and started reading, evoking the feeling I had three years earlier when reading *The Godfather*. I wondered if I would like other books and started looking around, asking librarians and teachers. By the end of my sophomore year, I was reading one book after another. I dropped my math major, signed up with an English advisor, and registered for extra literature courses. I even read the books the teachers had assigned (and I had skipped) in high school and became a fan of Thoreau, Emerson, and Shakespeare.

By the time I graduated with a degree in English education, I knew I wanted to do things differently from my English teachers. I needed and wanted to teach core books and classics, but I also wanted to give my students choices about reading all year.

Giving students choices about what they read and time to read those books through sustained silent reading (SSR) is the central concept of this book.

SSR is a program that has been important to me throughout my career and has grown in importance. In an age when even math tests require reading, SSR is a gift for both teachers and students. In fact, when I interviewed for my current job, I answered all the questions the panel asked me. When they asked, "Do you have any questions for us?" I only had one. "I have used sustained silent reading in my classes for years. Is it OK if I do that here?" The answer was yes and I took the job.

SSR has become part of my identity as a teacher and as a person. I've often overheard students talking about me, saying, "He's the one who has you silent read every day" or "He lets you pick the books you read." My students know they are going to read every day, and they know I am going to read with them. They see my books on my desk ("I didn't know English teachers read things like that!"), and they hear me talk about books all the time.

I don't want my students to experience the frustration and boredom I had experienced with reading. I am so thankful that I discovered how much I love reading, and for all that reading has given me. I want to offer my students similar opportunities, and to share with parents and teachers how the SSR program works in my classroom. I've written this book as if we were standing in the hallway between classes, chatting about reading, books, and students. Let's talk . . . .

○　　○　　○

Introduction

Why Use Sustained Silent Reading?

It was 1977, the first day of my teaching career, and my schedule consisted of three sections of a class called Basic Communications I and two sections of its sequel, Basic Communications II. Some students in these classes lacked interest in reading and writing, were learning disabled, or had been recommended for extra help by a prior English teacher. Most, however, had failed every other English class. For an English credit and graduation, I was their last hope.

As I waited for students to enter Room 211, the burden loomed large. What if I couldn't motivate them? What if they didn't earn passing grades? What if I couldn't find a way to teach them?

My background offered no help. My neatly typed student-teaching units on *The Grapes of Wrath* and *Huckleberry Finn* remained in the file cabinet. The curriculum for the Basic Communications classes required making our way through a series of workbooks. Having reviewed my teacher's edition, I could see how it led us through each workbook, page by page. I intended to do what I'd been told.

When the students entered the classroom, my fears were realized. Most showed up without pencils, paper, or interest. Most were quiet and filled the rows of seats from the back of the room. Some acknowledged me with a nod or a shy, "Hello." One slammed his backpack on the desk and asked, "You the new English teacher?"

"Yes, I am."

"I knew it. They always give these classes to the new guy."

"Why do you say that?"

"Nobody else wants to teach us. Like last year, I had that new lady and she failed me."

"Why was that?"

"Because English class sucks."

He laughed and most of the others laughed with him. Class had barely started and he had already succeeded in doing what he did best—making himself the center of attention. I would write his name, "Don," on several passes to the principal's office before the semester was over.

We settled in. I passed out the workbooks, loaned enough pencils to write names on the front of the packets, and gave instructions for the first three pages. When the bell rang, we stacked the workbooks on a shelf, and the students left the room.

By the end of the day, I was wondering how I would ever teach the way I wanted to and overcome the poor attitudes, histories of failure, and blank looks of boredom. They hated my class, and they hated school. I didn't know what I could do, but I knew I couldn't give up so early in my career.

Each day I passed out the workbooks and gave instructions. I tried telling stories to give some life to the lesson, but they weren't interested. We moved on, worksheet after worksheet. By the end of two weeks, I was depressed.

I remembered the discussions in the American Literature classes during student teaching. The short story collections and novels had sparked lively exchanges; final papers had been a joy to read. Now, discussions consisted of me talking while students looked at me. Or not. Writing assignments consisted of three-line paragraphs with no capital letters, no punctuation, and no main idea. I tried helping them as a group. I tried helping them individually.

One day, Tom—bless him for being so honest—said, "I know there should be some commas and periods in there somewhere, but I don't have any idea where. If I put them in and they're in the wrong place, I'll look stupid, so I just leave them out."

I'm sure others felt the same, but couldn't or wouldn't say it.

What could I do? How could I develop their confidence in themselves, and perhaps more important, some interest in what we were doing in class?

I spent the weekend trying to figure out how I could change something, anything, on Monday morning to help us all get through the next week. I remembered I'd heard another teacher talk about something called sustained silent reading. I decided to try it.

On Monday, I explained to each class, "We are going to start silent reading in class every day before we work in our packets. Choose a book from home or check one out from the school library tomorrow." I arranged with the librarians to help us look for books and by midway through each class on Tuesday, everyone had a book. We spent the remainder of class reading. On Wednesday, we read first, and then finished workbook pages. And each day after that, we read for the first 15 minutes, and then hustled to get through the daily lessons.

It didn't take long to see a change. Classes settled down sooner. They grumbled less about the workbooks. We even talked about the books they were reading.

It was better, but there were still problems. Kids left their books at home. They lost interest and complained about the books they chose. They fell asleep and couldn't remember what page they were on. Bottom line, it was still English class; Don had defined that in precise terms.

I still thought we were on the right track. With constant reminders, most students brought books to class; most remained quiet and read during the silent reading time. I don't know if research was available in the late '70s to tell me about the effects of SSR. If it existed, I didn't know about it, but within a month of starting SSR in my classes, I knew I was doing something that felt right.

During reading times, I sometimes looked around the room,

amazed at the faces, concentrating, trying to read and comprehend. They liked the idea of choosing their own books with quiet time to read them.

About this time, a new grumbling began in the room when I asked them to put their books down and get the workbooks off the shelf. They often asked for a few extra minutes. Sometimes I allowed it, sometimes I didn't. Then someone asked, "Could we read the whole period on Friday?"

I bargained. "If we read for 15 minutes every day, then work hard in our workbooks Monday through Thursday, we can read all hour on Friday." It was the first time I saw them truly excited as a group.

We read every day. They were remembering to bring their books. We talked about our books and shared funny stories and memorable characters. It took less time to get settled each day. Occasionally, someone would already be reading before the tardy bell rang. I was enjoying it, and that made me enjoy the rest of our work more.

One day, a note from the school secretary explained that every new teacher was required to have three formal, written evaluations. The principal would stop by my room for one period sometime in the next two weeks. Two days later, he walked into my classroom during the passing period.

When he sat down in a vacant seat, I was nervous. Things had been going well. I liked my students. I had developed a routine that gave me a sense of belonging within the school and within my own classroom. But he was the principal, and I was young, unsure, and untenured.

When the bell rang, I began with my usual, "Take out your books and let's do our silent reading." They settled in and we spent our 15 minutes reading. The workbook pages that day had some exercises on spelling and questions about the sequence of events in a short passage I read aloud to them. They answered the questions, and we had one of our better discussions about the reading passage. Class ended, and the students and principal left my room. I felt pretty good about what had happened and hoped my evaluation would be a favorable one.

A week later, a note arrived, asking me to stop by the principal's office during my planning hour. I sat down across the desk from him; he slid a copy of my evaluation to me. "Take this with you and look it over," he said. "If you have any questions, talk with me. If not, just sign it and put it in my mailbox.

"I thought it was interesting visiting your class," he continued. "You seem organized, and the students interact well with you." His tone indicated that something else was coming.

"I do have one question, however. I'd like to know about those 15 minutes at the beginning of class when the students are just sitting there reading. How do you justify taking that time away from them and their learning?"

I didn't know how to respond. I was so proud of how much the students had progressed, how their attitudes were more positive, how they seemed to be enjoying the silent reading, and how that spirit carried over into our work on the daily lessons. I mumbled, "I heard this was a good way to help students with their reading," but I knew that my disorganized and incomplete answer did little to "justify taking that time away." As soon as possible, I left his office, taking my disappointment with me. I knew I should have been able to give a better answer, but I still felt like the rookie and didn't have much more than a few bits of intuition to support my belief. Although my overall evaluation had been positive, his doubts about my reading program—my most successful activity—stung me.

That night at home, I worried about what I was doing. Was I really wrong in having the silent reading time? Was I wasting their time and my own? Was I misunderstanding my students and their work when I thought I saw improvement? And the hardest question—if this were wrong, what would I use to replace it and still get the positive results I was seeing from SSR?

The next day I started class with silent reading. My students, of course, knew nothing of what had happened in the principal's office, and I wasn't going to tell them. I wanted to read with them again and decided I'd continue silent reading until I had confirmed its value or found a better alternative. While they were reading that day, I again surveyed the room and watched their faces. They were engaged. They were interacting with words, they were thinking, they were learning. I realized that my principal's comment about the students "just sitting there reading" actually meant that, in his mind, I wasn't doing my job. I wasn't standing in front of them, "teaching" them. I wasn't writing notes on the board for them to copy. I wasn't probing them with questions, making them respond. What I was doing was sitting and reading, and perhaps even worse, enjoying it.

I decided then that we would continue silent reading every day. I would make sure we finished all the required lessons. I'd have them write book reports or give short speeches on their SSR books, so the books seemed more a part of the curriculum. I'd look for more reasons, more examples to support why silent reading was working.

I didn't have to wait long. David sat in the front row, right in front of me. My first impression of him hadn't been a good one. I'd watched him in the parking lot do a wheelie on his motorcycle and roar off down the street. He had put his helmet on first, but even that motion carried an attitude. When he walked into my class, I expected more of the aggression I'd seen on the motorcycle. I never saw it. He sat quietly in his desk every day. He was pleasant and turned his work in on time. I was pleased and relieved.

A couple of weeks after my meeting with the principal, I took roll at the beginning of class and began to read from a list of announcements of things that would affect students in the coming days. I was halfway through the list when David raised his hand.

"Do you think you could stop talking?" he asked. "We only get 15 minutes to read each day, and you're taking up a lot of our time."

"I'm sorry, David. You're right. I said we would read first, and I didn't do what I said. I'll save this until later, and we'll start our 15 minutes now."

He nodded. I'd solved his problem for him, and he was satisfied. He had no idea how big a problem he had solved for me. Students often say the right thing at exactly the right time.

David provided one of the first steps in confirming the silent reading program in my mind, removing doubts I'd suffered since my evaluation. If SSR was that important to David, it must be important to others, but I needed to find out exactly how important it was to them and why.

I created a list of questions (Figure 1) to survey students about their backgrounds in reading. From comments like Don's on the first day of class, I knew already that most of them hadn't done much reading and didn't like reading. I wanted more details about how silent reading could help them. I asked the questions aloud and had the students write answers to them. At the end of each class, I collected the papers and took them home that night. I got an education.

If students know that you are sincere and want the best for them, they will work with you, even though they may not like you or your class. Because we had talked frequently about the importance of English class and the skills I expected them to learn, and because the silent reading program had created a sense of interest and success in most of these students, they answered the questions honestly and fairly, with the usual comical responses. Overall, the answers gave me an insight into who they were as readers and where we needed to go.

As I read more than 100 papers that night, patterns emerged from the pages. These students, for the most part, had had little success in English class. Their answers to my questions made it clear that they needed and, in many cases, desperately wanted help in becoming better readers. Their answers confirmed for me that sustained silent reading was going to be one of the keys to giving them that help.

For the first question, I expected that most would say it had been quite some time since they had finished a book. That was an understatement. While some qualified their answers by saying the

Figure 1

Survey Questions for Students' Background in Reading

1. Before our silent reading program in this class, when was the last time you read an entire book?

2. How many books have you read for our silent reading program?

3. Does your family have a bookshelf in your home? If so, how many books are on it?

4. Do you have a bookshelf of your own? If so, how many books do you personally own?

5. Have you seen your parents/guardians read books? If so, how often?

6. Have you seen your parents/guardians read newspapers or magazines? If so, how often?

7. Have your parents/guardians ever recommended a book to you? If so, did you read it?

8. Have any of your friends ever recommended a book to you? If so, did you read it?

9. Answer the question below (A or B) that fits you best as a reader:

   A. If you don't read books regularly, what are some of the reasons you don't?

   B. If you read books regularly, what do you like about reading?

10. Do you like the silent reading program? Explain.

last book they finished was one a previous teacher forced them to read, more than half of the students stated either that they had never finished an entire book or that it had been so long, they couldn't remember when it was. While I understood that the distractions for high school students are many and powerful, I had imagined that most would have had a hobby or personal interest that would have inspired them to read a book or two occasionally. That was clearly not the case. They were not reading on their own and did not view reading as enjoyable or desirable.

When we discussed this in class, I had two further questions. First, I wanted to know what they did outside of school. The community we lived in was work oriented, so the most common response was that they had a job. Many said they worked almost every night after school, some logging nearly full-time hours. The second most common response was sports practice, followed by a variety of other activities, including homework and "hanging out with my friends."

Second, I wanted to know why they did not want to read on their own. "Not enough time" was the most common response. Because of their involvement in work and sports, their afternoons and evenings were often scheduled well in advance. "Reading is boring" and "There aren't any good books" were frequent answers. This discussion brought out problems with reading and mirrored the answers they gave to Question 9, Part A ("If you don't read books regularly, what are some of the reasons you don't?"), the overwhelming choice for that question. Time conflicts, distractions, and responsibilities in the home, on the athletic field, at work, and elsewhere were definitely more urgent than reading on their own.

To succeed at helping them become better readers, I would have to find ways to overcome both mental and physical barriers between these students and reading. Ideas came from answers to the other survey questions.

Most students reported that neither they nor their families had bookshelves in the home. Because books were not easily accessible to them, reading couldn't be a spur-of-the-moment activity. To read a book, they would have to take the initiative to find one. In most cases, that didn't happen.

For students with family or personal bookshelves, the difference was obvious. They were the better readers in the group and liked the idea of SSR from the beginning. A couple of them described reading at home with their families, a homebound version of SSR. However, most students had never seen their parents read a book and only slightly more had ever seen their parents read a magazine or a newspaper. Their parents seldom or never recommended books (although a few said they had read books based on recommendations from friends) and did not offer encouragement for reading at home. Reading, in most of these homes, simply did not exist and was not an important part of the family structure.

What I learned reading those papers that night was depressing. Obstacles to reading were huge, and my early attempts at an SSR program had been small. Students' attitudes were ingrained from years of experience; I had only 15 minutes each day to change those attitudes. It wasn't a fair conflict, but one final pattern in the papers made it seem that I might have a chance.

One question—"Do you like the silent reading program?"— stood out from the others. Nearly every student had complained about how difficult reading was, how boring it was, how every teacher made students write book reports, how students got in trouble for losing a book or library card, how hard it was to stay awake while reading. The list of complaints was long and resounding, until that last question.

Answers like "I didn't think I was going to like this, but it's not so bad" affirmed the program. Enjoyment of the current book or feeling more relaxed in class because of SSR time surfaced. One girl wrote, "If you're asking these questions because you are thinking about stopping the silent reading, please don't. I've really started to enjoy it, and I'm even reading my book at home before I go to bed."

The barriers to students' success in reading were real. I couldn't compete with the thrill of a football game or a wrestling match. I couldn't help pay for a new pickup or car. I couldn't replace family members and long-held attitudes. But the surveys had given me a better understanding of my students and their lives. I had much to think about.

Unfortunately, I didn't keep that stack of papers. I gave them back the next day in class, and we discussed what I had learned from their answers. While I knew SSR was going to be important to me and my students that year, I never guessed that day how important it would be in subsequent years, or that I would become such a strong proponent of it.

I never had the chance to convince my first principal of the value of SSR. He left at the end of the year to work in another state; however, I myself became convinced. Every English class I've taught in four different high schools for the past 27 years has featured sustained silent reading as the centerpiece of the classroom. Literally thousands of students have come to my room to read. They have been below-grade-level readers, average students, honors students, Advanced Placement students, and English as a Second Language students. Silent reading works for all of them. They've seen the magic that happens when they choose their own books, read them at their own pace, and share the joy of reading with their peers and teacher. Sustained silent reading is the single most important thing I have done for my students. I can't imagine teaching without it.

Part I

What Is Sustained Silent Reading?

1

Creating Lifelong Readers

Sustained silent reading is a time during which a class, or in some cases an entire school, reads quietly together. Students are allowed to choose their own reading materials and read independently during class time. Most programs encourage students to continue reading outside of class and permit students to change books if they lose interest. Most important, SSR allows an adult to model the habits, choices, comments, and attitudes good readers develop. Although most programs do not require traditional book reports, some do offer opportunities for students to talk or write about their readings. Although SSR programs share certain characteristics, teachers have adjusted the general concept to fit the specific needs of their students and schools.

Sustained silent reading is referred to by a number of different names across the country. In its purest form, FVR (free voluntary reading) allows students to read any materials they choose, including books, newspapers, magazines, and comic books. Programs include DEAR (drop everything and read), DIRT (daily independent reading time), LTR (love to read), USSR (uninterrupted sustained silent reading), POWER (providing opportunities with everyday reading), FUR (free uninterrupted reading), IRT (independent reading time), SQUIRT (sustained quiet uninterrupted reading time), WART (writing and reading time), SSRW (sustained silent reading and writing), and a host of other catchy acronyms and abbreviations.

First described by Lyman Hunt of the University of Vermont in the 1960s, SSR gained popularity in the 1970s. In the 1980s, many schools across the nation experienced rooms of quiet readers, although SSR was often criticized for the general lack of student accountability inherent in the programs. By the 1990s, SSR received strong competition from technology-based reading programs like Accelerated Reader software, which brought computer quizzes on selected books into the classroom. In the new millennium, the National Reading Panel reported that SSR programs were not an effective means of teaching reading, renewing a debate that has followed SSR throughout its history.

In spite of that report, interest in silent reading remains high, perhaps fueled by an increasing number of district- and state-required assessments and by the Elementary and Secondary Education Act (No Child Left Behind). These high-stakes assessments have left many teachers and administrators looking for successful, cost-effective ways to improve student reading. Worried about the "teach-to-the-test" mentality these assessments foster, some educators are concerned that students may become successful at taking tests but cease to enjoy reading. Because SSR is inexpensive and focuses strongly on reading for enjoyment, it may be the perfect answer. A significant number of research studies have examined sustained silent reading programs, evaluating their effectiveness with students from primary grades to graduate school (see Chapter 6), and most of these studies show that SSR is successful in promoting and improving student literacy.

What Researchers Say

The theory behind sustained silent reading is that if students read more and enjoy it more, they will become better readers, the same theory that drives the basketball player to stand at the free-throw line after practice each day and shoot 100 free throws. By the end of the season, he will be a better shooter, whether he has direct instruction or not. While practicing shooting, he will apply what he learns each day to the next day's practice. Readers are the same. As they read each day, they encounter new words, usage, sentence structures, and ideas. Each day adds to their total experience and makes the next day better. With increased practice, reading becomes easier and—this is important—more enjoyable. Like the basketball player and his team, readers in SSR classrooms share the reading experience with their classmates and teacher. They talk about their books, trade recommendations, and see fellow students and at least one adult engaged in the reading process.

Stephen Krashen of the University of Southern California, in his excellent book *The Power of Reading* (1993, p. x), describes free voluntary reading as "reading because you want to. For school-age children, FVR means no book report, no questions at the end of the chapter, and no looking up every vocabulary word. FVR means putting down a book you don't like and choosing another one instead. It is the kind of reading highly literate people do obsessively all the time."

Turning students into "highly literate people" is exactly what silent reading programs are designed to do. "Free Voluntary Reading is one of the most powerful tools we have in language education," Krashen says (1993, p. 1). He continues, "It will not, by itself, produce the highest levels of competence; rather, it provides a foundation so that higher levels of proficiency may be reached. When FVR is missing, these advanced levels are extremely difficult to attain."

Krashen believes silent reading programs are the most effective way to teach not only reading proficiency, but also all the skills related to reading. Success through FVR is based on what he calls "the complexity argument." Language, he says, "is too complex to be deliberately and consciously learned one rule or one item at a time" (1993, p. 14). This argument applies to grammar as well as vocabulary. "Not only are there many words to acquire, there are also subtle and complex properties of words that competent language users have acquired" (p. 14). Minor differences in usage may cause words to have very different meanings, presenting a challenge that students will not be able to meet by studying words from vocabulary lists alone.

To add to this complexity, "when we acquire a word we acquire considerable knowledge about its grammatical properties. With verbs, for example, this includes knowing whether they are transitive or intransitive, what kinds of complements they can be used with, and so on. Very little of this knowledge is deliberately taught" (Krashen, 1993, p. 14). He points out that

> vocabulary teaching methods typically focus on teaching simple synonyms, and thus give only part of the meaning of the word, and none of its social meanings or grammatical properties. Intensive methods that aim to give students a thorough knowledge of words are not nearly as efficient as reading in terms of words gained per minute. In fact, Nagy, Herman, and Anderson (1985) argue that picking up word meanings by reading is 10 times faster than intensive vocabulary instruction. Their suggestion is not to do both instruction and reading—the time is better spent in reading alone.

Jim Trelease, author of the national bestseller *The Read-Aloud Handbook* (2001), makes a strong case for parents and teachers to encourage and participate in reading aloud with students. His research is thorough and convincing. One of the most compelling chapters is "Sustained Silent Reading: Reading-Aloud's Natural Partner." "SSR is based upon a single simple principle," Trelease (2001, p. 107) says. "Reading is a skill—and the more you use it, the better you get at it. Conversely, the less you use it, the more difficult it is." Does SSR work? According to Trelease, it does:

> When the International Association for the Evaluation of Educational Achievement (IEA) compared the reading skills of 210,000 students from thirty-two different countries, it found the highest scores (regardless of income level) among children:
> • Who were read to by their teachers daily
> • Who read the most pages for pleasure daily. (p. 107)

Moreover, the frequency of SSR had a marked impact on scores: Children who had it daily scored much higher than those who had it only once a week. American NAEP assessments found the identical pattern for the nearly twenty-five years NAEP has been testing hundreds of thousands of U.S. students. The evidence for reading aloud to children and SSR is overwhelming—yet most children are neither read to nor experience SSR in the course of a school day. (p. 107)

While recognizing that the research is important, any teacher who has been in a successful silent reading program knows the magic that happens when students are engaged and reading. I've experienced it for years, and it is always exciting to see another teacher discover that joy. A teacher who observed those good results in her classroom produced one of the finest books ever written on the subject. Nancie Atwell, author of *In the Middle* (1987), changed the way thousands of teachers approach reading and writing instruction. She realized that teachers model behavior and attitudes, whether they intend to or not. She lists the negative things teachers model (and students learn) about reading:

- Reading is difficult, serious business.
- Literature is even more difficult and serious.
- Reading is a performance for an audience of one: the teacher.
- There is one interpretation of a text: the teacher's.
- "Errors" in comprehension or interpretation will not be tolerated.
- Student readers aren't smart or trustworthy enough to choose their own texts.
- Reading requires memorization and mastery of information, terms, conventions, and theories.
- Reading is always followed by a test (and writing mostly serves to test reading—book reports, critical papers, essays, and multiple choice/fill-in-the-blank/short answer variations).
- Reading somehow involves drawing lines, filling in blanks, and circling.
- Readers break whole texts into separate pieces to be read and dissected one fragment at a time.
- It's wrong to become so interested in a text that you read more than the fragment the teacher assigned.
- Reading is a solitary activity you perform as a member of a group.
- Readers in a group may not collaborate: this is cheating.

• Re-reading a book is also cheating; so are skimming, skipping, and looking ahead.
• It's immoral to abandon a book you're not enjoying.
• You learn about literature by listening to teachers talk about it.
• Teachers talk a lot about literature, but teachers don't read.
• Teachers are often bored by the literature they want you to read.
• There's another kind of reading, a fun, satisfying kind you can do on your free time or outside of school.
• You can fail English yet still succeed at and love this other kind of reading. (p. 152)

Atwell then used these ideas to help her create a student-centered project that would teach this "other kind of reading." She calls it the reading workshop, and the rules she created give a good picture of what her class looks like during the workshop and how a sustained silent reading program works:

1. Students must read for the entire period.
2. They cannot do homework or read any material for another course. Reading workshop is not a study hall.
3. They must read a book (no magazines or newspapers where text competes with pictures), preferably one that tells a story (e.g., novels, histories, biographies rather than books of lists or facts where readers can't sustain attention, build up speed and fluency, or grow to love good stories).
4. They must have a book in their possession when the bell rings; this is the main responsibility involved in coming prepared to this class. (Students who need help finding a book or who finish a book during the workshop are obvious exceptions.)
5. They may not talk to or disturb others.
6. They may sit or recline wherever they'd like as long as feet don't go up on furniture and rule no. 5 is maintained. (A piece of paper taped over the window in the classroom door helps cut down on the number of passers-by who require explanations about students lying around with their noses in books.)
7. There are no lavatory or water fountain sign-outs to disturb me or other readers. In an emergency, they may simply slip out and slip back in again as quietly as possible.
8. A student who's absent can make up time and receive points by reading at home, during study hall (with a note from a parent or study hall teacher), or after school. (1987, p. 159)

Atwell's approach has some restrictions (no magazines), which technically remove it from the free voluntary reading category but make it a good example of how a teacher can modify sustained silent reading to meet her own needs and those of her students. Atwell notes that students are free to "sit or recline wherever they'd like," which is an example of another option. Some teachers provide couches or beanbag chairs in the classroom. Some create reading corners or lofts, while others have students remain in their seats. Many factors would become part of a teacher's decision about organizing a room for SSR.

The Flow Experience

When I read and hear about ways teachers have adapted SSR to fit their needs, I'm amazed at what a democratic process it is. Used successfully throughout the United States and in many other countries, with students of every age group and every reading ability, it's not a one-size-fits-all garment, but with a little stretching here and a little tucking there, it can be made to fit any situation.

What provides this utility? The major premise behind any sustained silent reading program—that reading should be enjoyable. Students still need assigned readings from the core curriculum. They need discussions and quizzes, but not on everything they read. SSR offers students a chance to make choices and to take control of part of their education, a very powerful concept for them. Teachers work with students in a different way, as a mentor would: assisting in book selections, helping students past difficult parts in their books, acting as a sounding board for student reactions to their reading.

We all love to do things we enjoy. No one has to teach us to enjoy an afternoon at the beach splashing in the waves. No one has to instruct students that "hanging out with friends" is fun. We seek out things we enjoy and avoid things we don't enjoy. Students who learned about reading based on Atwell's list of negative modeling probably don't enjoy reading and don't seek it out. However, I suspect a high percentage of students who sat in her reading workshops in the 1980s are avid readers today.

If sustained silent reading has an ultimate goal, it would be to create lifelong readers. SSR gives students the choices to explore authors, genres, and topics worth their reading time. I often refer to a character, the Good Adult Reader, when we talk about making choices and learning to become better readers. The Good Adult Reader becomes a generic model of what I want them to become. I use the Good Adult Reader as an example and ask questions like "What do you think a Good Adult Reader does when he needs to find a new book?" "What do you think a Good Adult Reader does when he doesn't understand a passage he has just read?"

As coach of the cross-country team each fall, I recognize similarities between "coaching" sustained silent reading and coaching distance running. At the beginning of the season, runners are out of shape and still in a summer frame of mind. As they become fit, feel the success of improving their times at races, and share the "runner talk" on the bus and in team meetings, their motivation for running becomes less external—me giving them the workout for the day—and more an intrinsic sense of wanting to feel the motion as they float over the hills in the park on a beautiful October afternoon. Perhaps the most satisfying part of my coaching comes on those days when I am driving home from school and see a runner who graduated four, five, or six years ago jogging down the street. I honk. The runner waves, and we both smile. SSR is the "lifetime sport" of the academic world, and I wish I could drive past the houses of former students, see them reading, and honk.

If SSR is such an enjoyable activity, what makes it so? The best theory I've seen is the work of University of Chicago psychologist Mihaly Csikszentmihalyi. In his book *Flow: The Psychology of Optimal Experience*, Csikszentmihalyi (1991) interviewed hundreds of people from around the world and asked them to describe how they felt when they were involved in an activity they enjoyed. He talked with chess players, musicians, rock climbers, tennis players, surgeons, and many others, and based on their accounts of what it felt like to do what they were doing, I developed a theory of optimal experience based on the concept of *flow*—the state in which people are so involved in an activity that nothing else seems to matter. Flow occurs when a person challenges herself and meets success in the challenge. (p. 4)

In other words, if the challenge is too difficult, frustration and anger may result when she fails to reach the goal. If the challenge is too easy, boredom sets in and she loses interest in the challenge. Keeping the challenge balanced between frustration and boredom is a natural state for people to seek, according to Csikszentmihalyi. We see it every day when children play games and adults solve crossword puzzles or learn to play a new piece of music. When a person is able to maintain that balance, enjoyment results, and it creates a sense of "forward movement" (p. 4). Csikszentmihalyi writes,

Enjoyment is characterized by this forward movement: by a sense of novelty, of accomplishment. Playing a close game of tennis that stretches one's ability is enjoyable, as is reading a book that reveals things in a new light, as is having a conversation that leads us to express ideas we didn't know we had. Closing a contested business deal, or any piece of work well done, is enjoyable. None of these experiences may be particularly pleasurable at the time they are taking place, but afterward we think back on them and say, "That really was fun," and wish they would happen again. After an enjoyable event we know that we have changed, that our self has grown: in some respect, we have become more complex as a result of it. (1991, p. 46)

When students participate in sustained silent reading and enjoy books they have chosen, reading becomes a flow activity. Watching students during SSR time reveals that most, if not all, have become so involved in their reading that they are no longer aware of others. They laugh, they frown, they shake their heads; occasionally, they blurt out in amazement or anger because of something a character has said or done. It may seem humorous, but it clearly shows they have become involved in their reading and have found the balance Csikszentmihalyi describes as forward movement.

My colleague Judy Barnes told me, "The most remarkable of these experiences for me was watching a girl read last year. As she sat silently in her chair, tears were running down her cheeks. She continued to read, completely absorbed, and not self-conscious about the tears."

Csikszentmihalyi's analysis of flow experience includes two other aspects directly related to SSR. The first, he says, is concentration:

> In normal everyday existence, we are the prey of thoughts and worries intruding unwanted in consciousness. Because most jobs, and home life in general, lack the pressing demands of flow experiences, concentration is rarely so intense that preoccupations and anxieties can be automatically ruled out. Consequently, the ordinary state of mind involves unexpected and frequent episodes of entropy interfering with the smooth run of psychic energy. This is one reason why flow improves the quality of experience: the clearly structured demands of the activity impose order, and exclude the interference of disorder in consciousness. (p. 58)

Reading and writing impose this order. Students often say, "Oh, I was really getting into my book" when SSR time ends. They like the feeling of getting that involved, and after they experience it a few times, it becomes easier and easier to return to that level of concentration with each reading session. For some, that level of involvement defines a good book.

Csikszentmihalyi called the other aspect of flow experience "the transformation of time." In his studies, he discovered that

> one of the most common descriptions of optimal experience is that time no longer seems to pass the way it ordinarily does. The objective, external duration we measure with reference to outside events like night and day, or the orderly progression of clocks, is rendered irrelevant by the rhythms dictated by the activity. (1991, p. 66)

Students in SSR classes often report feeling like this. Any reader who has glanced up, surprised to see that it is 1:00 in the morning, knows exactly the feeling. The nature of sustained silent reading is such that it not only fosters the kind of challenge that leads to forward movement, but also sets the stage for concentration and the transformation of time explained by flow theory. While it is easier for researchers to measure student progress in vocabulary, grammar, or fluency, greater reading enjoyment is what will lead a student to lifelong reading. SSR creates the flow activity that supports enjoyment. Any teacher who has shared SSR time with students has seen it happen, often as quickly as the second week of the program.

The flow experience is very real, but it can pose one danger for teachers. As Csikszentmihalyi discovered in his research, flow is universal. It crosses cultural and economic boundaries with ease. It doesn't discriminate based on age. I long ago lost track of the number of times a student cleared his or her throat or tapped on a table to bring me out of the depths of a book, only to discover that our 12 minutes or 15 minutes of reading time had suddenly turned into 26 minutes or 30 minutes. Although it may be embarrassing for a moment and may lead to some scurrying to catch up with the planned lesson, it provides a different sort of modeling for students to see. Adults get engrossed in their reading, and students need to see that.

Research shows that SSR works in teaching second-language students. Two experiences had taught me this even before my impressions were confirmed by Krashen, who wrote, "FVR is also, I am convinced, the way to achieve advanced second language proficiency" (1993, p. x).

I had experienced this myself in 1981, teaching at the American School of Lima, Peru. As soon as I stepped off the plane at Jorge Chavez International Airport, I realized I was in trouble. My one year of high school Spanish (far too many years in the past) wasn't going to help me, so I quickly did what I thought was the right thing. I hired a tutor. Rosanna was an excellent teacher, and we went through pages in her textbook and wrote sentences and vocabulary words in a notebook. I studied hard, but still found myself hoping that when I was out in the city, the waiter or store clerk who helped me would be the one who spoke at least a few words of English. That was seldom the case, and I ended up pointing at pictures on the menu or writing prices on a piece of paper.

Then one day I picked up a copy of *El Commercio*, the largest daily newspaper in the country. The first day, it took an hour, with frequent references to my dictionary, to read the banner story. Within two weeks, I could read the front page in an hour, and within two months, I could read the newspaper much as I would at home. The biggest benefit, however, was in the vocabulary and sentences I learned. The banner news was the Falkland Islands war, so I learned about rockets, tanks, ships, and other military terms. Suddenly, I could understand conversations on the street—real people talking, not just words from the vocabulary lists in Rosanna's grammar book. I learned to follow World Cup soccer scores, the progress of the Peruvian national women's volleyball team, local authors' book signings, and a host of other events and issues that were the topics of daily conversations. By then, every person I met was my language teacher. I talked with taxi drivers, shopkeepers, and people on the street. My time in Lima was immediately more enjoyable.

The second experience occurred on a trip to Kiev, Ukraine. My wife, Peggy, and I were walking near the central plaza when we met Oleg. He asked if he could walk with us and practice his English. He explained that he was a language student and could speak eight languages, but English was the hardest for him to practice. Because this was during the time of the Soviet Union, most tourists in Kiev were from Eastern bloc nations. He had plenty of chances to practice his Slavic languages, but few chances to speak English. We spent the afternoon walking through Kiev, talking with him. When we parted, he asked if we would like to walk again with him and his wife in the evening. We agreed and set a time to meet. Before he left, he asked, "Do you have any American novels with you?" We did. "Would it be possible for you to give me some? I can't buy them here. I have English textbooks, but I want to read novels, so I can understand the juice of the language."

I went back to the hotel and opened my suitcase. I took out all the books we had, even removing my bookmark from the one I was reading at the time. I could always get others; it was clear these books were more valuable to him.

When we met near the statue of Lenin, I handed him the stack of books. His eyes brightened. The books would supply hours of work and pleasure for him.

Although he gave me a beautiful cross-stitched Ukrainian shirt, the look on his face when he saw the books was a gift, one that became more important to me through the years. When I give students sustained silent reading time in my class, I am passing on that gift. If they are going to become lifelong readers, they need to "understand the juice of the language."

2

Encouraging Student Progress

After my initial attempts at silent reading with my Basic Communications students, I decided I needed to try different ways of encouraging students' reading progress. My classload changed to include not only Basic Communications but regular sophomore English classes as well. I decided to use silent reading in the classes to see its effects on them. Though generally better readers and less reluctant to pursue reading, results for these sophomores were strikingly similar to those of the Basic Communications students.

After several weeks of silent reading, I conducted the earlier survey I had used with struggling readers. The sophomore English students reported many of the same benefits from SSR. They were more interested in reading and enjoyed it more. Many wrote about feeling more confident with their writing and said their vocabulary and spelling were improving. While I was happy to hear this, I still wanted to experiment with the program structure.

Accountability

During my first five years of teaching, I believed students needed to be accountable for everything they read. Written book reports were due on a regular basis. They were short reports, but I wanted to be sure students were actually reading the books and understanding them. I asked them to note the title and author, do a brief plot summary, and discuss character development.

With more than 100 book reports every four weeks, the workbook packets for the Basic Communications students, and the core curriculum writings for the sophomore English students, I was buried in paperwork, spending too much time grading papers and not enough time planning good lessons and activities.

The students felt the paper pressure, too, complaining that writing so many book reports was boring and a waste of time. I cringed when I heard that, because getting them away from the idea that "reading is boring" was a major premise for starting SSR.

I took a closer look at the reports, which were blurring together in my mind. They all sounded alike, and why shouldn't they? I had given them all the same formula for writing the report. They were bored writing them; I was bored grading them.

I decided to simplify the process. Instead of using the book report outline, I developed a short form with nice, neat lines for commenting on the main character, the conflict, the theme, and the plot. Easier for them to write and for me to grade, but the form quickly lost its novelty. It was still a book report and still had to be written and turned in by a certain date.

One day, I was grading book report forms and noticed that the writing seemed more formal, more developed than I expected from several students. A quick trip to the library revealed that they were copying from the blurbs included on the back of the book. While I had tried to do them (and me) a favor by simplifying the reports, I had simplified them to the point that the back cover commentary could serve as the book report. I had watched them reading the books in class. I had talked with them about the books. I was certain they had read the books, so why would they cheat on the reports? How could I have them respond to the books without creating paperwork that could destroy the enjoyment of our silent reading program?

I decided to try oral book reports. I asked students to choose a character, assume that persona, and give a report to the class by talking in first person. They could use a prop, but it wasn't required. I asked them to bring their books to show during the report and to include one minute of reading from the book as part of a three- to five-minute presentation. For many students, this was a refreshing change. They enjoyed the chance to talk about their books, and they saw it as better than writing standard reports. It was also much easier and less time-consuming for me to grade. I developed a rubric checklist, gave each student a copy, and simply rated each part of the report as presented. I could grade the reports in class and return them at the end of the hour.

It seemed to be a better situation, but oral reports pose unique problems. Many students, like many adults, dread the thought of speaking in front of peers. For them, oral book reports are torture, and the suffering clearly shows on their faces and through their body language. Some felt it was so difficult that they simply looked at me and said, "Give me a zero on the report. I read the book, but I'm not going to stand up in front of the class and talk about it." While I understand the importance of having students speak in class and learn the art of public speaking, the stress was defeating the purpose of SSR.

Also, the class found the first three or four book reports engaging, but after that, their attention waned, and few students listened to the remaining reports. At approximately five minutes each, oral book reports for an entire class use about three class periods, time that can't be used for SSR or core curriculum lessons. Done twice each semester, 12 days would be used during the school year for reports that few students heard.

As I struggled with the idea of accountability for silent reading books, I combined book report styles. Students completed a long, written book report, a short report on the form, and an oral report in front of the class. That gave more variety to the program, but didn't completely eliminate the problems of reports that sounded like blurbs and students who refused to talk in front of the class.

Any form of book report I used violated two of the central issues in sustained silent reading. First, by asking students to comment on character, theme, and conflict, I had unthinkingly required that their books be novels. The format of the report ruled out story collections, poetry anthologies, and most nonfiction. While I had stood in front of my students and said they could read any book in any genre, my forms didn't live up to that promise. Through the years of my program, I have seen that although most students choose novels for SSR, many prefer other genres or choose a mixture of genres throughout the year. I found it strange that during those years of book reports, no student ever complained about this limitation. They complained about writing the reports, about speaking in front of class, but not about the biased structure of the book reports.

Second, the book reports required that all students respond to their books at the same time, either by handing in the written report on a specific day or by giving their oral report on one of the three assigned days. Problems with this are obvious. Many students who read at a slower pace did not have their books finished by the due date. Others, who read faster, had completed two or more books during the time and then had trouble choosing which book to use for the report or had already returned the book to the library and didn't have it on hand for the report.

When the reports were due on a certain day, at least one student in each class finished her book two weeks before the deadline, wrote the report, and announced, "There, I finished my book and report. Now I don't have to read until the next grading period." While she might know the guidelines of SSR and know she needed to bring a new book the next day, I had trouble getting a student to participate once she had completed the "required" book.

These problems were distracting us from my goal of increasing their interest in and enjoyment of reading. If I wanted them to become lifelong readers, book reports were not going to be the road to my goal.

That's when I created the Reading Record, a very simple list with three columns (explained in more detail in Chapter 3). For each book read, the student simply lists the author and title and records the number of pages read. This may or may not be the same as the number of pages in the book, depending on whether she finished the book. This format simplified the report process, both for students and for me. All their work is listed, and they and I can quickly see how much they have accomplished. As the year progresses, a feeling of pride grows as the lines fill with book titles. Their efforts and accomplishments as readers become tangible on the Reading Record.

Even though I liked the Reading Record from the start, and it gave us more freedom and time to read, I initially felt a little guilty about it because it removed much of the accountability from the process. However, I have used a version of the Reading Record for several years now and am pleased with the results. Recording their progress takes only one minute per book, and they are ready to move on to the next book. Simple and painless, it places the emphasis exactly where I want it.

When teachers see the Reading Record, they ask, "How do you know they actually read the books?" Bottom line is, I don't. On the other hand, did I know they actually read the books when they were copying blurbs off the back covers or writing paragraphs that could have easily come from "borrowed" book reports? Even today, with computer-assisted programs like the Accelerated Reader software to provide quizzes, won't students find ways to take the quizzes without reading the book if it is a book they don't want to read? Yes, they will. In fact, the Internet has opened a new realm for less-than-honest students through cyber cheating (Flannery, 2004; Gardiner, 2001a). Any teacher today who thinks he hasn't graded dozens of book reports or research papers downloaded from www.schoolsucks.com, www.ez-write.com, www.cyberessays.com, www.schoolpapers.com, or scores of other cyber cheating Web sites needs a loud wake-up call.

In instituting the Reading Record, I was concerned that students would not have the opportunity to express their feelings about a book. They could write about it in their journals or choose that book for one of the core curriculum literary analyses, but I wanted something more immediate, something quick, easy, and effective. I had heard about other teachers using book talks and decided to try that.

They were an instant hit. I model the process by telling about a book I am reading or have just finished. I then invite anyone else from the room to talk. With no time limits, they can volunteer to talk or not; they can summarize the plot, talk about a character, or react to their books in any way they want. Others may ask questions. It can take 5 minutes or 20 minutes to do a book talk, depending on how much students have to say and how much time we can afford in class. Book talks have provided the perfect oral balance to the Reading Record.

I have developed one other means of connecting with students and their books, a one-on-one quick chat. Because my students have to bring their books with them to class every day, I often see their reading books under their arm as they walk in the room. "Hey, I read that book last year and really liked it. What do you think about it?" or "I've heard that is a good book. Do you think I should read it?" I use this same approach as I circulate around the room, collecting or returning assignments or distributing handouts. These brief encounters, combined with observing them reading in class and reviewing their Reading Records, provide more useful information about them as readers than any book report formats I've ever used.

Simplifying the book report was necessary for another reason. In the last chapter, I cited a quote from Krashen in which he called SSR the "foundation" for other learning. If SSR is the foundation, and if teachers are required by district or state curriculums to teach other core materials, those lessons provide more than enough opportunities for group discussion, quizzes, tests, and literary critiques. What the SSR program should provide, then, is more time for reading, specifically more time for reading what students choose to read for enjoyment. Through this choice, SSR balances the "teacher-selected" core curriculum materials.

Time for Reading

From the beginning, I believed in daily reading (discussed further in Chapter 4), but I struggled with two aspects of organizing that time. First, I experimented with where the reading time should fall within the class period. SSR always works best as the lead activity. Reading in the middle of class seems to disrupt the entire flow of the lesson. Reading at the end is nearly impossible. With the core lesson completed, "class-is-over" thinking permeates the room. Occasionally a lesson dictates that we start at the beginning of class; if time is left, I've sometimes announced, "OK, you can have your silent reading time now," a hard sell. Someone invariably announces, "It just doesn't feel like silent reading time." Free reading clearly works best at the beginning of the hour, explained in more detail in Chapter 3.

The other consideration regarding time is how many minutes to allow for reading. I've tried everything from 10 minutes to 30 minutes, which seem to be the extremes. In 10 minutes, too many students are just getting into a reading rhythm when I ask them to stop. In 30 minutes, many students lose their focus, and it becomes difficult to complete the core lesson. I tried varying the amount of time, using, for example, 10 minutes one day, 20 minutes the next day, 15 minutes the next day. We are creatures of habit, and I found that students work better when they know exactly what is ahead of them. Therefore, I've settled on 15 minutes as the ideal time for my program, giving enough time to settle in, enjoy some good reading, and complete our daily lesson. Students develop the 15-minute habit quickly, and some have even timed me, arguing if they are "cheated" out of reading time.

Reading Materials

When I talk with teachers about their SSR programs, one of the greatest variables seems to be how they deal with the types of reading materials allowed and the amount of access to reading materials.

Traditionally, free voluntary reading allows students to read anything—books, newspapers, magazines, comic books, or whatever they choose. Other SSR programs, like Atwell's, restrict reading materials to books with a story line or to those on book, author, or topic lists. While teachers need to structure silent reading programs in ways that best meet their needs, too many restrictions may defeat the central purpose of SSR, which is increasing student enjoyment in reading.

I've allowed students to read just about everything at one time or another, but I excluded magazines, newspapers, and comic books from SSR early in my career. Several issues make those three forms of reading less desirable in the classroom, and the problem is not their content or writing style. Rather, all three are not very long, so they require frequent resupplying. Because students read these materials so quickly and finding new material takes more work on their part, they are more apt to run out of reading material in the middle of a reading session or arrive at class empty handed. With these shorter materials, readers never seem to settle in and take ownership of their reading choices. If I have a box of magazines or a stack of newspapers in my room, students may simply grab one so that they have something in front of them during reading time. They are meeting the requirement of reading, but not the spirit of SSR. I want them more involved in their reading choices.

Newspapers, especially, and to a lesser degree magazines and comic books, also have a built-in "noise factor." Newspapers tend to fall apart and spill over the floor. As students turn the large pages, they rustle and tear, distracting other readers. Students are far more likely to turn to another student to share an article or cartoon when reading magazines and newspapers, thus violating that student's right to "sustained and silent" reading time. These may seem like minor problems, but they quickly compound to create an atmosphere acceptable for talking or laughing during SSR.

Another concern with magazines, newspapers, and comic books is they present the material in short bits. I realize that these are what Good Adult Readers often read, so when I present this restriction to a class, I might say, "I want you to choose a book that you can read from day to day. I know some of you might want to read magazines, newspapers, or comic books, but I have a feeling that most of you read those at home on your own time. I enjoy magazines myself and have half a dozen subscriptions that I read regularly, but for silent reading, I'll bring a book every day, and I want you to do the same." It is a simple explanation, but I can't remember a single student complaining about that guideline.

When I first heard about sustained silent reading, the sustained part was explained to me as an uninterrupted time for reading, a single unit of time. Over the years I've expanded that definition. I want the sustained concept to last beyond the 15 minutes in class, to carry over to the times they read in the evening, over the weekend, or on vacation. A book that goes with them in their backpacks provides continuity in their reading. Although students might deny that they read outside class time, most do when they find the right book. I'll often survey students on a Monday morning or on the first day back from a vacation. "How many of you read in your silent reading books over the weekend?" "How many of you took your book with you on vacation and read?" In general, half the students in a class will raise their hands. That's a good result, but it also enables students who don't raise their hands to realize that others are reading at home on their own time. It might be the first time they understood this. Next time, they might take their own books on vacation.

The other issue related to reading materials is access. Students must have books if they are going to be readers. If I require them to read books, I must provide access to books, but I don't have to provide the books. I've read about and seen some excellent classroom libraries, but I don't have one. It may make more sense in an elementary school setting where students are reading many short books and are continually replacing them, but in a high school, it is not necessary, and perhaps, not even desirable. I know many SSR teachers will disagree with me on this point, but this is a conscious decision, one I'm comfortable with for several reasons.

Classroom libraries cost money. I'm aware that grants, PTA donations, and book clubs can help fund them, but initial cost is only one issue. If books are torn, dropped in mud puddles, chewed by dogs, or decorated with graffiti, they must be replaced. In addition, student interests change as new authors and titles are published. Because every school in the nation has a library that spends thousands of dollars each year updating collections, I choose to take advantage of that excellent resource.

I have worked in four school districts in two states and in two countries. In every location, the librarians have smiled when I explained my silent reading program. Librarians want students in their facilities, and I want my students there, comfortable in the library. I want them to learn how to search for books. I want them to talk with librarians who understand my program and know why my students are there. I want my students to carry their library cards and use them. And since my ultimate goal is to help students become lifelong readers, who better to model that behavior than school librarians? They are the epitome of Good Adult Readers.

A classroom library means I, or someone else, must assume the role of librarian and monitor the check-out/check-in process, which would certainly coincide with SSR time and interfere with the sustained and silent part of our program. Even if books are set out and offered on an honesty or "read it and bring it back when you are finished" basis, the movement of several students to the bookshelf would delay the beginning of reading time and their return to their seats would provide further distraction to readers. Instead, I send students to the library one or two at a time. Thus, shuffling books, requesting help, and checking out books disturb no one. They return to class with a book and join the other readers.

Every year several students will ask, "Can I just leave my reading book in here so I don't have to carry it with me?" They can't. I want them to take ownership of their books, even if they don't personally own them. The books need to become a part of their day, a responsibility they assume as part of their growth as readers. If they leave their books in my room, they can't read them at night or in study hall or while they wait for a ride home after school. I want them to carry books with them, and I want other students to see them carrying books. If they can just grab books off my shelf (either their own or from a classroom library), it is too easy to forget about the books when they leave my room. It is also too easy to look at a few pages of one book today and randomly look at a few pages from another book tomorrow. Choosing a book should be more purposeful. Good Adult Readers may browse through several books in a library, bookstore, or friend's living room, but they eventually settle on a book and begin sustained reading.

Another reason I don't have a classroom library is that I can't meet the interests and reading needs of the more than 100 students who would use it. Even if I can provide 200, 500, or even 1,000 books, I still won't have the book that explains how to replace brake shoes on a car or that re-creates the life of the latest Academy Award–winning actress. I could never meet all the reading needs, interests, or ability levels in my classroom, but I can help them take responsibility and find books they need.

Although I don't have a classroom library, I do provide multiple paths of access to books. Students may bring them from home, buy them, borrow them from friends, or utilize the excellent human and literary resources of the school library to find books. That freedom is the best kind of access.

Modeling Silent Reading

When my cross-country runners show up for practice each fall, they know they will be getting hot, thirsty, and tired. They also know their coach will be feeling the same. I do every workout I assign to them, and they appreciate it.

Whether it is five miles, eight miles, repeat runs on a hill, or speed work on the track, I haven't missed a workout with them in 10 years. They see me run, and watch me share in their struggles and feel their successes. They know I understand their situation, and they feel comfortable talking to me and asking questions about their running.

Of course, if one of them ever complains about a workout, I simply say, "I'm three times your age, and I just finished that work-out." End of complaint.

The same situation exists in my English class. We have silent reading every day. Every day I read with them. They see me read. They hear me talk about my book. They walk by my desk, pick up my book, and ask about what I'm reading. Most students do not see an adult read a book very often, if at all. My most important job in the classroom is to show them how an adult participates in reading and talking about reading.

Research supports the value of modeling silent reading. After analyzing several SSR programs, Pilgreen wrote,

> When teachers, administrators and classroom assistants read, they projected their conviction that reading was both pleasurable and worthwhile, disenfranchising students of the notion that reading in school was nothing more than a school task. Students came to see that the adults valued reading, and they, in turn, were willing to try it themselves. (2000, p. 13)

The single most important factor in determining the success of an SSR program is the teacher's attitude. If SSR is truly to be sustained silent reading, everyone, including the teacher, needs to participate for the full time of each session. When that happens, habit takes over, and the program begins running itself in just a few days. A teacher who outlines the program, enforces the guidelines, and sets the example creates a silent reading program that is a winner.

Modeling silent reading means I read with them every day, not just when it's convenient for me. It would be hypocritical of me to tell them they can't do homework during SSR time, and then grade papers, check e-mail, organize my desk, or do any of the hundreds of things it would be nice to complete during that time. But why would I want to? I'm selfish. I get to sit and read the book of my choice every day. Every year a student realizes this and says, "We read every day, but you read in every class, don't you?"

"Yes."

"Must be nice."

"It's a sacrifice, but for the sake of your education, I'll step up and take the responsibility."

They laugh, but they also see that I enjoy the reading enough to be involved several times each day, week after week, month after month. I do, sometimes, feel guilty. I get paid to read books. And in the fall, it's even worse. I get paid to read during the day, and after school, I get paid to run with some of the most motivated students on campus. Someone ought to report me.

3

Organizing and Running an SSR Program

When I talk with teachers who are interested in silent reading, they often ask similar questions: How do you start an SSR program? How do you explain it to students so they understand what you want? How do you monitor it so you know what is going on?

In recent years, many teachers have discovered the power of videotaping themselves and watching the tape to see exactly what is happening in their classrooms. It helps them understand their actions and the reactions of their students. Perhaps the easiest way for me to explain the questions teachers have about SSR is to create a written videotape of what occurs in my classroom the first few days of each semester as I establish the silent reading program. For me, a successful start would go something like this:

Day 1

"Good morning. I'm Mr. Gardiner, and I teach the yearbook class and two newspaper classes. I also teach two sections of this class, Sophomore English, and we're in Room 206. Is everyone in the right place? Good. Let me call roll. Please correct me if I mispronounce your name or you go by a name different from the one on the school record."

I take attendance quickly, briefly introduce the class content, and then quickly move on to explaining sustained silent reading.

"Sophomore English is required for graduation from Billings Senior High School. The school district curriculum for this class dictates that we have several writing assignments including a personal experience essay, descriptive paragraphs, book reviews, and others, and that we complete several required reading assignments. For example, we'll be reading selections of poetry and short stories, a play by Shakespeare and another by Sophocles. All of these readings and writings are in the textbook I'll give you during the last half of class tomorrow. Right now, we need to talk about and start the most important thing we'll do in this class, the silent reading program.

"I imagine many of you have done silent reading programs in the past, so this is not all new, but let me explain how it works here. First, you will need a book by tomorrow. It can be any book that you choose. You know the topics you like to read about. You know the authors you like best. You know the level of difficulty you can handle. I just met most of you a few minutes ago, so I can't pick books for you. That wouldn't be fair for you or me, so your homework for tomorrow is to get a book.

"Where will you get this book? That's up to you. Maybe you have a book that you got for Christmas or your birthday, and you haven't had time to read it yet. This would be the perfect time. Maybe your parents have a book that you have wanted to read, or maybe a friend has talked to you about a book that he or she thought was really good and suggested you read it. Now would be a great time to do that. Maybe you like to go shopping and want to go buy a book tonight. That would be great, but no one will have to spend any money on this program. The public library has thousands of books sitting there waiting for you, and our school library has thousands more. In fact, the librarians have signed us up for the first 15 minutes of class tomorrow. If you have a book at home, bring it. If your friend has a book you want to read, borrow it. If not, bring your library card tomorrow, and we'll go to the library. Our librarians are excellent at helping students find books. They all understand the silent reading program and can point you in the right direction.

"The book you choose for this program should be a book that you personally want to read. Don't choose a book because you think it will impress me or because it will impress your parents. That might keep you interested in reading it for a day or two, but if that is your motivation, it will leave quickly. Choose a book you want to read. You might choose it because of the topic or the author or because it has a great title or the blurb on the back sounds interesting. Any of those would be reasons to try a book, because they are reasons that come from you. Any questions at this point?"

"How many books do we have to read?"

"Good question and thanks for asking it, because several of your classmates were sitting here thinking exactly the same thing. First, I prefer to word the question, 'How many books do we get to read this year?' and I hope you'll see why I say that very soon. But the real answer to your question is you'll read as many books as it takes to get from tomorrow to the final bell on the last day of school."

"But how many books is that?"

"I can't answer that. Some of you will choose short, easy books. Others will choose long, difficult books. This isn't math class. I can't take books and count them as units and put them into some formula that makes it all come out equal for everyone. Each of you has your own reading ability and your own reading interest. That's the beauty of literature, but it's impossible for me to compare all the variety of books that are out there for us to discover. I've taught silent reading for a lot of years, and other students who have been in my classroom showed me I was wrong to assign a certain number of books. What did those students do when I did that?"

"They picked out all the short books."

"Exactly, and when I assigned a certain number of pages, they immediately looked for books with large print and lots of pictures. Choosing books because they are short or because they have large print makes no more sense than saying, 'I'm going to read all the red books in the library this year, and next year I'll read the blue books.' The number of pages, the size of the print, the number of photos—those are not the reasons to choose a book. There is only one reason to choose a book—because it is the book that you want to read right now.

"I hope that helps you understand my comment about needing enough books to last until the end of the year. If you need something more specific, maybe I can help. I've kept records of what students have read in past years, and there is an amazing consistency. When I take all the Reading Records (don't worry about those now, I'll explain them in a day or two) and figure an average for a class, it ends up about seven books per student per semester. It might be 7.2 books one semester and 7.6 another, but it's somewhere near that magic number of seven. You look like you don't believe me. It's true. I know somebody is sitting in this room right now, and please don't raise your hand unless you really want to, but someone is sitting here thinking, 'I haven't read a book in seven years, and now he wants me to read seven books in one semester. Who does he think he is?' Somebody's thinking that, right? You're smiling. OK, maybe several of you are thinking that. Let me tell you this. The students sitting in these chairs last year at this time had the same question in mind, as did the students the year before that, and guess what? They averaged seven books per semester.

"Does that mean that every one of you will read seven books?"

"No. You said that was an average. So what if I only read one book?"

"That's right, it's an average, and average means that some will read more and some less. What if you read only one book? That might be OK, if the book is long or difficult or both. But what if you surprise yourself and read more than 7 books? Many in this room will. I don't know which of you will, because I don't know you as readers yet, but I will. In fact, I'll go so far as to say that at least eight people in this room will read more than 10 books this semester. Yes, and at least five will read 15 or more books. Three of you will read about 20 books and one will read between 25 and 30 books this semester. Again, I don't know who will do this, but it happens in this class every semester, and I haven't seen anything so far that tells me this semester is going to be any different."

"Nobody can read 25 books in a semester."

"Four years ago, I had a student who read 56 books in one semester."

"Yeah, like some geek who needs to get a life."

"Actually, she was a very cute girl who got good grades, acted in the school plays, scored high on her SAT tests, and made off with thousands of dollars in college scholarships. I'm just guessing that at this moment, she feels the extra time she spent reading was worth it. Now, she was truly the exception, but I wanted you to see what is possible in this program. I don't expect any of you to read 56 books, but again, most of you will read somewhere around 7, and that will be an excellent accomplishment.

"We'll read every day, almost always the first 15 minutes. I told you at the beginning of class today that the silent reading is the most important thing we'll do in class this year. That's why it comes first every day. Between now and June there will be only a few days when we won't read. There will be days when you will have to meet with your counselors for registration, days when we have a major test, and days when we are watching a video related to one of our core books. On those days, we may have a shorter reading time or no reading time at all. I'll try to keep track of those days and give a few extra minutes on days when our lesson is short so that we make up the silent reading time we missed. On test days, you will need to have your silent reading book with you so that if you finish early, you can read while your classmates finish their tests. How are we doing now? Other questions?"

"What kind of books do we have to bring?"

"That's your choice, with a few exceptions. You could read a novel, a book of short stories, a collection of poems, a biography. Any of those would be great. I do have a couple of requests. Please don't bring textbooks from another class, magazines, newspapers, comic books, or books that are a collection of comic strips. Those are great things to read, and I encourage you to read them on your own time, but for English class, bring a book that has a story to it and is the right reading level for you. You're in high school now, and I think you can pick something that will be worth your time and keep you interested.

"You might have a favorite topic that you want to read about, or you might have an author that you read before and would like to read again. That would be great. Speaking of authors, who do you think is the most popular author I see over the years in this silent reading program?"

"J. K. Rowling?"

"Yes, she's popular now, but only in the past few years. I'm guessing many of you have read a book or watched a movie, a scary movie, by a man whose books I see in here every year."

"Stephen King?"

"He is the all-time champion of the silent reading program. Have any of you read a John Grisham book? I see his books in here a lot, along with authors like Danielle Steele, Tom Clancy, and Michael Crichton. Have any of you read the Chicken Soup books? I'm seeing those the past few years. Of course, I also see students reading Hemingway, Steinbeck, and Shakespeare. Yes, people choose to read Shakespeare on their own and you could, too.

"I have a question for you. You've listened to me talking about silent reading, and some of you might be advanced foreign language students. Do you think it would be OK to read a novel in Spanish or French in this class?"

"No."

"Why not?"

"Because this is English, and you said we couldn't bring books from other classes."

"Yes, this is English class, but what I said was don't bring a textbook from another class. It's silent reading time, not study hall. Leave the textbook, but if you are capable of reading a novel or poems in another language, feel free to bring them. There is plenty of research that shows that silent reading is a big help in learning another language. OK, any other questions?"

"Do we have to get up in front of the class and talk about our books?"

"No, although some of you will want to, and I'll be happy to make time. Just let me know when you want to do that. We will have days called book talks, and I'll talk a little about a book I've read or the one I'm reading at the time. Anyone in the room who wants to share comments about a book may do so. There are no requirements about book talk and no grades. You may have a minute or two to just tell us about your book and answer questions if anyone wants to know more.

"We won't be giving oral book reports to the class. I've done that many times, and what I've learned is that after the first three or four, everyone loses interest and doesn't hear a word of the remaining reports. That's bad enough, but the worst part is giving oral book reports takes about three class periods, and then we miss too much silent reading time.

"Written book reports are the same. They take too much time, and students who are reading a lot of books and enjoying them want to keep reading more books. I've also learned that if I ask you to write a lot of book reports, those of you who read at a slower pace are more apt to copy blurbs off the cover or download book reviews from the Internet to help you keep up. I don't believe that is helping you become a better reader. I want us to focus our energy on reading books. It's awfully quiet in here right now. Are you waiting to see what the catch is because we don't have to give book reports?"

"We always have to write book reports or talk to the class."

"You won't in here. There will be times when we need to write about our reading as part of the district curriculum. In those cases, we'll sometimes write about an assigned reading, and other times, I'll give you a choice of writing about one of the core reading assignments or choosing to write about your silent reading book. So while there won't be mandatory book reports on the silent reading, you will have the option of using your book on some writing assignments, if you choose.

"You'll hear me talk about a make-believe person I call the Good Adult Reader. This person is the reader I want you to become. To get you there, I'm going to treat you like an adult reader. You get to choose your own book. You get to read it at your own pace. You get to talk about it with a friend or the whole class if you want to. You get to take it home and read it before bed. You get to take it with you in the car on vacation. You get to quit reading it if you lose interest. You get to read two books at the same time if that interests you. In other words, you get to take control over this part of your education and make decisions about using this time I'm giving you. I'm only asking one thing: Please use the time wisely."

"What do you mean, use it wisely?"

"Read something that means something to you. A few years ago, I had a student who read a flight instruction manual every day. Some of you might think a manual would be boring reading, but he wanted his pilot's license very badly. He read every day and at the end of the year, he completed his test and earned his pilot's license. About two years after that, he earned a commercial pilot's license and became one of the youngest pilots in the state. I'd say he used his silent reading time wisely, wouldn't you? He took control of his own reading and became a Good Adult Reader.

"That's enough for today. I have more to say about silent reading, but it can wait. I've talked about our reading program and this class, but I still don't know much about each of you. Take out a sheet of paper. We have 10 minutes left, and I want you to write a paragraph telling me something you want me to know about you. That way I will know at least one thing about each of you when we come to class tomorrow. Just imagine that we met each other and are talking. I've told you about my class, and now you take a minute and tell me about you. Give me your paper before you leave class."

The students write for 10 minutes.

"The bell is about to ring. What is your assignment for tomorrow?"

"Bring a reading book."

"Or?"

"Bring a library card."

"Right. Don't forget. Silent reading starts tomorrow, and everyone in the room will read."

Day 2

My classroom has tables that seat four students each. I allow students to choose their seats on the second day, and we make the seating chart from their choices. I explain that they may sit where they want as long as they participate in silent reading and don't interrupt anyone who is speaking during class. The tables work very well for most classroom activities, especially small group peer editing, so I like teaching with them, but I know that four friends sitting close together can lead to what I call "small group discussions." I've learned over the years that once a group starts talking, they usually don't stop, so I give one warning, and on the second offense, I move those students to different parts of the room. It usually only takes one moving for the rest of the students to realize that they need to follow the format of the room, if they want to keep the seat they have chosen. As long as they respect each other and me, they may sit where they choose, and the seating chart is only to help me learn their names and help if we have a substitute teacher.

We take two minutes to set up the chart. Then I ask them, "What was your assignment for today?"

"Bring a reading book."

"Yes, and how many of you brought a reading book from home?" Usually about half will have a book in hand.

"I assume the rest of you want to take advantage of the offer to go to the library now. Let me quickly review what we talked about yesterday. For silent reading, you may bring any book you choose. It could be a novel; a collection of short stories; a collection of poems; a biography; or a nonfiction book such as a travel story, an adventure, or a how-to manual. You need to have the book here every day from today until the last day of school. We'll read every day, with the few exceptions I outlined yesterday. When you finish one book, you need to get a new book for the next day. Any questions about what we need to do?"

There might be a question or two to clarify something, but most groups are anxious to go, if for no other reason than to get out of class and walk to the library.

"Let's go then. If you have any problems finding a book, ask any of the librarians. All of them know about our silent reading program, and they are experts at helping you find a book that suits your interests. Those of you who brought a book may make a choice. You may browse for books you might want to read later this year, or you may sit in the library and read while the rest of us check out books. We'll all come back to class in 15 minutes with a book."

With the help of the librarians and me, most students are able to find a book in just a few minutes. Some may need to request new library cards or take care of fines from last year, but most quickly get a book and return to class. I usually let them read for 20 minutes that first day (those who brought books get an even longer reading session) and then stop them.

"Let's stop your reading there for today. I'm glad you all got books and were able to get started on the silent reading program. As I said yesterday, I believe this is the most important thing we do in this class. Now that you've read once, you know how it will work. We'll sit silently and read the first 15 minutes of each class, just like you did today.

"I like to do survey questions. I've got my first question for you right now. I know you only had a few minutes to start your book today, but how many of you, on first impression, think you have found a book you are going to enjoy? Good. Almost everyone raised a hand. I'm glad to see that. That is the key to this whole program.

If you don't enjoy your book, the reading time won't be much fun. Yesterday I talked to you about that person I call the Good Adult Reader. What do you suppose the Good Adult Reader does when she has a book she doesn't like?"

"Quits reading it."

"Maybe. But sometimes it's not that simple. For example, there are some books I read that might not be my favorite, but I know I need something from that book. Maybe it is a book about helping my daughters get financial aid for college. I may not enjoy the reading, but I know I need to learn what I can to help them, so I stick with that book. On the other hand, if it is a book that I've chosen to read for enjoyment, and I find I'm not enjoying it, then, yes, I quit. I've been reading for a long time, so I'm getting better at choosing the books I'll like, but I still don't get it right every time. Neither will you. I recommend you give it a few reading sessions, and if you find you don't like it, let's get you a new one. I know some of you are wondering what will happen if you quit reading a book. Will that mean that you lose all the time you spent on it? No, it doesn't, and tomorrow I'll show you how you get credit for reading part of a book. That's enough on silent reading for today."

I then check out the textbooks and review the table of contents, so students can see the units we will be reading, discussing, and writing about. They have now seen that silent reading comes first, but they also know we will be reading poems, short stories, essays, plays, and novels that come from the core curriculum list.

"These selections from the textbook are our required readings. We'll have quizzes on them, write literary analyses on them, discuss them, and have unit tests at the end of each section. That will be quite a bit of work for you, but I hope you can see one other important aspect of the silent reading program now. If the textbook writings are chosen for you, the silent reading serves as a balance, because you get to make the decisions about that part of class yourself.

"Now that you have your textbook and reading book, add a notebook and pen or pencil to the list and know that you will need all four of those items every day. Reading and writing are what this class is about, and you'll need those four things with you to be successful here."

Day 3

"Take out your silent reading books and let's read."

This is the first day for students to bring all four required items, and usually one or more will not have a reading book. While I don't stock a classroom library for several reasons, I do have a handful of short story collections and student anthologies that make good single-session books for emergencies. I'll give a book to any student along with the request, "Please remember to bring your silent reading book every day." I quickly walk around the room to check that each student has a book to read, then settle in with my own. We read for 15 minutes and then stop.

"Let's pause there for today. Remember you are free to read in your book outside of class. You can read in study hall or at home before bed, and all the pages you read count for your silent reading for this class.

"On the first day of class, I told you I would show you how to keep track of your reading. I have a very simple form called a Reading Record. I'll give you a copy today, and I want you to keep it throughout the whole year. I'll pick it up every six weeks and give you a grade for your reading. When I give it back each time, I'll have a red line drawn on it to show how far you got each six weeks, and you just add more books to it for the next time.

"Look at your copy. Let's fill out the top right now. Write your name first, then on Line 1, write the title and author of the book you picked yesterday. Notice that the column on the right is for pages. Please don't write 'All' or 'To the end' there. I want a number there to tell me how many pages you read from the book."

"But you said we didn't have to read a certain number of pages."

"That's correct, but I do want to know how many pages you read. I've read hundreds of books, but I won't know every book that each of you brings to class. Putting the page numbers there helps me learn about you and what you are reading. And it lets you see very clearly the progress you are making as a reader. Also, do you remember when I said there is a way for you to get credit for reading part of a book?"

"Yes, how does that work?"

"You write down the title and author; then, in the column under Pages, you write the number you read. For example, if you read the first 52 pages of a 210-page book and lost interest, you would write 52/210. That would tell me you read those 52 pages and stopped there. Some of you may feel the need to explain why you quit, and if that's the case, you may write me a note in the margin, but you don't need to do that. I have already given you permission to stop, if you think that is what should happen. If we are going to get you to be a Good Adult Reader, I have to trust you to make that decision. If you stop reading a book, what do you need to do next?"

"Get a new book."

"Exactly. Then you write it on the next line and we continue like that through the year. The other way the page column helps us is at the six-week grading period. It would be nice and neat if on the last day of the six weeks, all of you finished your books right at the end of reading time, but that's not realistic. On that day, each of you will be in a different place in your book, so you'll tell me you read, for example, 165 pages in your book. I'll look over your Reading Record, draw a red line beneath your last entry, and return it. For the next six weeks, assuming you finish that book, your next entry would list the same title and author, but under Pages, you would write 166–382. That way you get credit for each part of the book you read in the correct six weeks.

"You don't need to make an entry for each day. You only need to make an entry each time you finish a book or on the final day of each six weeks. This way we keep record keeping to a minimum and reading time to a maximum. I've tried to make this as simple for both of us as I can."

"I'm still confused."

"What's that?"

"If we don't have to give book reports, and we don't have to read a certain number of books or pages, how do we get a grade for this?"

"It's actually pretty easy. I've tried several different point values and have settled on 60 points each six weeks. That makes the silent reading approximately equal to a major unit test from the textbook or just slightly more than one of the formal writing assignments usually scored on a 50-point basis. I take the 60 points and divide it into two sections. When you get your Reading Record back, it will have a top number out of 30. That number represents the quantity of reading you did. Since there isn't a specific number of pages or books to read, I can't just count totals for this grade. I look at the books you choose and how difficult they are, check to see how many pages you read at that difficulty, and then consider how I think that matches your skills and interests as a reader. This is difficult for me at first, because I don't know you well, but I'll quickly learn a lot about you as a reader when we talk about books and I see you read and discuss the required readings from the textbook. I'll admit this portion of the grade is subjective on my part, but I'll always give you the chance to come talk to me if you feel I treated you unfairly. I'll listen carefully to what you say, explain my decision, and we'll find a common number that we can both live with. I think you'll feel I treated you fairly, but if not, we'll talk about it.

"The second number, the one on the bottom, is very objective. Those 30 points are based strictly on participation in silent reading during class. If you bring your book to class and read every day, you get 30 points. It's that simple. If you forget your book, talk during reading time, work on homework, or write a note to a friend, I'll subtract five points each time. The math is easy. If you read every day, you'll have a 30 on the bottom and very likely a 30 on the top for a

60 total and an A+ on a major grade for this class. However, say you are a fast reader, read at home, and record a lot of pages. You might get a 30 for the top score, but if you forget your book three times, you would get a 15 on the bottom, meaning a total score of 45 or a C for the period. All I'm asking is for you to choose a book you want to read, bring it every day, and read. It's an easy A, and if you choose the right book, it should be a fun A."

Day 4

"Grab your silent reading book and let's start reading. I see several of you are already reading. That's great. You don't have to wait for me. Since you know we'll read first thing every day, you may start as soon as you are ready. In fact, that's one sign that you have found the right book. I said the key to this program is finding a book that you enjoy, and I hope that you find one that is so interesting to you that you actually look forward to getting here so you can read it. This is our third day of reading, and if you find that you are not looking forward to reading the book you have, give it another day or two and then you might consider finding a new book. Let's read."

We read for 15 minutes. For the first several days, I move around the room to check that each student has a book. Usually by the third day, most have picked up the routine and start reading immediately. Occasionally, one or two students will procrastinate, taking extra time to find their books or shuffling through a notebook as if they are looking for something. I quietly ask them to leave the notebook until later and wait beside them while they get out a book. As we read, I glance around the room to see who is engaged in reading. If anyone is not reading or is writing, nodding off, talking, or otherwise distracted, I walk quietly to that student and redirect him or her. Almost always, the student resumes reading.

By Day 4, students usually begin to make comments about what they are reading. I get questions about my own reading book, or questions about what else I have read. "Have you ever read this book?" is a very common question as a student holds up his own book. If I have, I offer an opinion. If not, I ask the student to tell me a little about it. In just a few seconds, we set the scene for later book talks we'll enjoy as a group. A quick exchange reinforces the idea that reading and talking about books really are central to my class. I've taken the time to comment on a student's book of choice; often that helps a student confirm the choice.

"Let's pause your reading there for today" is the way I end a silent reading session. The word "pause" perhaps reminds them of stopping the VCR to get a snack, and they know we will return and push "play" again the next day.

"Set aside your reading books for now. Take out your literature textbooks and let's look at the short story on page . . . ."

The 15 minutes of silent reading have created an atmosphere of literature in the room. They have been working with words; thus, it's an easy transition to writing, reading the textbook, or discussing a story, poem, or essay. It is as if the 15 minutes of reading are the equivalent of the warm-up and stretching done by an athlete before practice or competition. After silent reading, their minds and bodies are settled in for the second activity of the day, whatever that might be, and they move on easily. In fact, this ease of transition may be the strongest response to my principal from years ago to "justify taking that time away from them and their learning."

As anyone who has ever taught a class knows, it can take several minutes for a roomful of students to get out books and focus on the day's work. If that process done cold takes three or four minutes, and if students are still thinking about who they saw in the hall, what happened last hour, or a long list of other topics, they aren't engaged. Even if their books are opened, they haven't focused on reading and writing. More time passes as they do the mental stretching needed to gain that focus. I'm guessing this process takes as much as half of what could be silent reading time. I also believe that students who have done the mental warm-up of silent reading move more quickly and smoothly through the rest of the lesson and easily make up the class time devoted to SSR. The benefits of SSR for improving vocabulary, spelling, grammar, writing, and reading are documented in countless studies, but this very important tool for getting students into the mind-set of working with words and ideas won't be reflected in research. The transition to this class, this hour and then from the first activity to the second activity to the third activity is critical for every teacher who wants to get the most from time spent with students. Rather than distracting us from our work with core curriculum activities, SSR is the pathway into and through them.

The Second Week

By the sixth or seventh session of silent reading, the process becomes routine. Often it only takes a quick "Reading books, please" to get class started, and several times I've had classes in which "Let's pause there for today" is the first time they hear me speak. I've had dozens of classes who came into the room and simply started reading on their own with no direction from me.

During this time, students start monitoring themselves. If someone is ruffling through a backpack, tapping a desk, wiggling feet, or whispering, another student will likely correct the perpetrator. It might not be as friendly as my reminder, but a "Shut up" or "Knock it off" from another student usually restores the "silent" to SSR.

Another comment I hear frequently at this stage is "I can't believe how fast your class goes. It never seems like we're in here for an hour." SSR automatically breaks the class period into at least two parts, and I often split the second part again. When I taught at Jackson Hole High School in Jackson, Wyoming, we had a schedule of 90-minute blocks, four periods each day. Teachers learned quickly to plan lessons with as many as four or five activities per block. I liked the sense of movement that style created, and I stick to it today. Silent reading becomes an activity that helps students stay with me for the hour.

During the second week, I'll still do a quick survey at the beginning of class to see that each student has a book and correct the situation if a book is missing. By now, students know I'm serious about SSR and have already developed the habit of carrying a reading book, a major goal of my program.

"Good Adult Readers have a book around all the time," I tell my students. "Some have one book at home, one book in the car, one book in a briefcase and read whichever is closest. I always have a book with me. If I'm waiting for the doctor or dentist, I have a book. If I'm waiting to get the oil changed in my car, John, my mechanic, knows I'll be reading when he comes out to tell me my car is ready. If I'm waiting to pick up my daughter after swim practice, I'll have the dome light on in the car. If I'm backpacking, I have a small, light book tucked in the outside pocket of my pack. There are hundreds of good books I want to read, so I don't want to waste time. If the doctor isn't ready for me, I'll read a chapter. If I get caught in a storm when I'm camping, I'll listen to the rain hit my tent and think about something Thoreau, Muir, or Abbey wrote. Then, when the storm is over, I'll hike again."

In this second week, I survey the students again about the books they are reading. "We've been reading in class every day for seven days now. How many of you still think you have found a good book for you? Good. Almost everyone. If you have some doubts about your book, or find that you really aren't enjoying it like you thought you would, remember that you are free to get a new one. If it hasn't grabbed you by this point, I'd think about looking for a different choice. Remember, you can quit this one without any penalty. Just list it on the Reading Record, note how many pages you read, and find a new book."

After I've set up the program in these first few days, I monitor each day to see that everyone has a book, and I check during the reading time to see that every student is reading. Occasionally, I find a student who thinks he has played the game long enough and sneaks out homework or starts writing a note to a friend. I walk to his side and remind him, "There is only one thing we can do during silent reading time. Remember that half of your silent reading grade is based on participating every day." For most students, that stops the problem.

It is rare that a student will resist getting involved in silent reading beyond the second week. One or two students out of five classes might push it that far, but soon they look around and see a roomful of readers. The same influence that has frustrated parents throughout time, "But everyone else gets to go to the concert," kicks in. That resistant student realizes that truly, "everyone else is doing it," and most often, joins the crowd. The one student in several hundred who absolutely fights SSR over an extended period of time stands out in memory in the same manner as the true, incorrigible discipline problem every teacher encounters a few times in a career. I've moved students across the room to keep them from bothering readers. I've taken points off Reading Records until there weren't any more points to deduct. I've held students after class for one-on-one conferences about their behavior, but I've never had to send a student from the room over silent reading violations.

During more than two decades of SSR, over 3,000 readers have taken a seat in my classes and read an estimated 40,000 books. I've enjoyed every day I've spent with them. Tomorrow, I'll have my book in class again and join my students in 15 minutes of silence and reading.

Part II

What Do People Say About Sustained Silent Reading?

4

Common Questions About SSR

Throughout the many years I used SSR in my classroom, I received numerous questions from parents, students, and other teachers about the program. Many of the questions come up repeatedly and others are unique, but all bring up interesting and valid concerns and ideas about SSR. Since the publication of my article "Ten Minutes a Day for Silent Reading" in the October 2001 issue of *Educational Leadership*, I have received even more questions and many, many e-mails wanting to know more about silent reading. Samples of the questions I received and my short answers to each one follow.

Q: How do you find time to do SSR in addition to the core curriculum requirements?

A: Because my students know we will begin every class with SSR, they come in and settle down right away. In each class, several students will be reading even before the tardy bell rings. Occasionally, I have classes in which the entire group has already started reading, and I simply join them after I take roll. The time students spend reading gets them in a working attitude so that when we change to the lesson for the day, they are already warmed up, and we move quickly and easily into the activity. Because of this smooth transition and the ease of moving on, I believe several minutes of the reading time is made up. Combine that with the reading that happens while I am taking roll, and I don't think I lose any class time at all. The full hour is productive, and students' attitudes are good. Also, by changing activities after 15 minutes, I automatically change the pace and focus of the class each day. Students like having a change during the class period. I teach my lesson; we all get to read; everyone is happier by including SSR.

Q: How can you be sure everyone is reading every day?

A: I can't. Nor can I be sure that every single student listens closely to each word as we read *Julius Caesar* aloud in class or that every student completely understands each variable for punctuating dialogue when I demonstrate it on the white board. It's not realistic to expect that. Students are human beings with myriad concerns that may or may not be part of my classroom. I can encourage and direct attention, but I can't guarantee they will be with me every step of the way. I can monitor the room, however, and I frequently wander through the aisles, checking to see who is reading. Often, I quietly visit with a student about a book. As I read, I glance around the room. After two minutes of reading time, anyone who makes eye contact with me is not engaged. I may motion to them, or get up and visit with them if it is a lingering problem. To be honest, I never see the faces of the majority of my students during reading time. They get involved immediately and stay involved until it's time to stop.

During reading time, one of my jobs is to model an adult reader. Sometimes students laugh at me when someone quietly stands at the door waiting for me, and I don't have a clue the person is there. Yes, students also laugh at me when I get involved in my book, and we go 5 or 10 minutes over the normal time. So every day, I have to balance my duty as a room monitor with my role as a reading model and my own personal love of reading. Over the years, I've learned to read deeply, yet keep an ear out for sounds in the room. Anyone whispering or shuffling papers is not engaged in silent reading, nor, unfortunately, are those sitting nearby. I firmly believe in the "silent" part of silent reading.

Q: If you don't have students write book reports, how are they accountable for SSR books?

A: First of all, I don't think students need to be accountable for everything they read. As an adult reader, I don't want to take quizzes on every magazine article or novel I read. I just want to take from them what I want and need. Second, I hold students accountable for other reading, and SSR needs to be purely for enjoyment. From our core curriculum materials, students write character sketches; analyze theme, conflict, and setting; summarize plot; and discuss style. Core assignments provide sufficient practice in literary analysis. I want SSR to be used for reading, not writing reports, and I want SSR books selected by personal choice, not for book reports.

Having said that, some creative ways of doing book reports don't take much time and fit the general attitude of SSR programs. For example, we created a program at Billings Senior High School called Read It Forward. Reading teacher Terra Beth Jochems was inspired by the main character in the movie *Pay It Forward*, who believed that if he did three good deeds for other people and those people did three good deeds, a wave of happiness and goodness would spread throughout the world. Jochems translated the concept into reading: When students found a good book, she asked that they pass the book on to others. They enjoyed the program, which she called Read It Forward. Eventually, she wanted to expand beyond her classroom, so computer teacher Vince Long created a Web site (http://senior.billings.k12.mt.us/readitforward) that allowed students to write a short commentary on a book, rate the book, and submit the review for others to read. The site has become popular, and hundreds of students have taken the time to Read It Forward.

Q: Do you give students a reading list?

A: I never have. I want them to learn to choose and reject their own books. Our core curriculum lists required books, so I want SSR to balance that equation with student-centered reading. No reading list would meet the personal needs of the varied students who walk into my classroom. It always fascinates me to see what students choose when completely free to select reading materials. More than once, I've borrowed a book from a student after he's finished it. I think the freedom to choose is a vital aspect of SSR.

Q: Have you ever censored a student's book choice?

A: Never. There have been times when I've thought, "That's not the book I'd prefer that student read," but generally, if the book is the right connection for the student, she will read it and quickly move on, often to what I might term a "better" book. If the student has chosen a book just for shock value, she likely won't enjoy the reading and will drop it in a day or two. Through 27 years of SSR and thousands of student-chosen books, I'm very pleased with what students read and how enthusiastic they are about their choices.

Q: What if a student reads one Stephen King book after another?

A: I'd write a compliment in the margin of his Reading Record. Many of those books are 700, 800, or 1,000 pages long, a major achievement for a student reader. Once, a boy read three or four Stephen King books in a row. His mother came in to talk with me. "When are you going to make him read something besides Stephen King?" she asked.

"For the silent reading program, students are free to choose their own books," I replied.

"But since he's been in this reading program of yours, Stephen King is all he'll look at."

"What did he read last year before this program?"

"Well, he didn't read at all, but I'm concerned that he won't look at anything but these Stephen King books."

"If he wouldn't read at all last year and he's on his fourth book this year, aren't we winning?" I asked. Eventually he will read all of Stephen King's books, or he will get tired of Stephen King and move on to other authors the way all good readers do.

Q: But why don't you require them to read the classics?

A: There are three answers to this question. First, we require them to read the classics through a core curriculum full of selections that would meet the "classics" category. Any student who graduates from our district has read plenty of Hemingway, Steinbeck, Whitman, Frost, Dickinson, and Shakespeare, to name a few. To require books from that same list for SSR eliminates the change of pace the program offers. It would also change the SSR program from student-centered to teacher-directed, thus removing the vital choice so important to helping students become good readers. Trelease expresses a similar idea:

> An interesting thing happened to the classics: About the only people in this country who read them are teenagers—and only because they have to. Don't misunderstand me: I am awed by the great minds and great writing. I read and revere the classics, but everything I've seen in the last thirty-five years indicates we are misusing them in schools, to the point that we are undoing much of the good they were created to accomplish. We've got ninth-graders reading books like *The Great Gatsby* before they're old enough to bring a frame of reference to them. And to make things worse, the books are dissected until every trace of appeal has been lost. (2001, p. 140)

Second, one thing that has always amazed me is the number of students who, given freedom of choice, pick the classics. At any time in a class, I generally find students with classics they heard about from friends in other classes or books that have been on a family bookshelf for years. SSR doesn't eliminate or discourage reading classics, it just lets students choose them at the right time.

Third, in certain situations, requiring more core curriculum material would guarantee failure. Some students have spent years struggling with the classics and have had no success. Perhaps they have found other styles of writing that lead to success and keep them interested. What if a student wants to read about how to repair auto body damage or how to build a Web page or how to cook a Pakistani meal? Aren't those topics worth reading and learning about? Leaving SSR book selection open to choice creates balance for all students. Those who want more classics get them; those who want other types of literature can get them too. Through this process, students provide the work of choosing and rejecting books. I provide the time, the space, the encouragement. I treat them like adults capable of making decisions about their own education. The focus is on them; it's student-centered learning at its best. If only it were this easy to solve other educational problems.

Q: If students read their books outside of class, does that count as part of the SSR program?

A. They get full credit. That is the essence of SSR. If students are interested enough to read in study hall, on the school bus, in bed, or elsewhere, they are well on their way to becoming lifelong readers. There is no more important skill or habit that we, as educators and parents, could hope to encourage.

Q: Where do students get their books?

A: I did a survey of students this year, because I had never formally asked this question. Fifty-eight students completed the survey, and responses indicated that 537 total books had been read, an average of 9.2 books per student (Figure 4.1). I was not surprised that most of the books came from the library. It is convenient, and our librarians are very helpful. What did surprise me was that nearly one in five books was purchased, indicating how much students (and parents) value the silent reading program.

Figure 4.1

Survey of Students in an SSR Program

Source of Book	Number/Percentage of Books Acquired This Way
1. Student bought the book.	97, or 18% of books read in program
2. Student borrowed the book.	100, or 19% of books read in program
3. Student brought the book from home.	117, or 22% of books read in program
4. Student got the book at a library.	223, or 41% of books read in program

Note: Survey completed by 58 students; 537 total books read.

Q: Do you allow students to sit on couches, beanbag chairs, or the floor when they read?

A: I think the idea of a couch or beanbag chair is a nice gesture, but in my mind, it creates another level of monitoring for a teacher. If students leave their regular seats, they will usually arrange to sit next to a friend and the temptation to visit, pass notes, copy homework assignments, or hit each other is greater than most can overcome. Some teachers successfully use couches and beanbag chairs with SSR, but they have to keep a close watch on students. One year, my students wanted to spread out on the nice, carpeted floor during SSR. That worked out well because they were still separated and could read with no problem. My classroom floor now is concrete, so no one asks to lie on the floor to read. Occasionally, students ask to move into a corner or otherwise away from other students to help them concentrate, and I allow that. My experience with high school students is that most of them are fine in their regular seats. I prefer that as well, because SSR seems more like part of the regular class rather than a separate activity with a different seating arrangement. This decision, like most regarding SSR, should be made by each teacher based on what works best in the individual classroom and what keeps the silent reading program moving smoothly and efficiently. In my mind, keeping the rules and format of the program as simple as possible is usually the best plan.

Q: Should students be rewarded with prizes for their reading?

A: I know we give prizes for all sorts of things in education, but I don't support prizes for SSR. Individual teachers may find that younger students or classes of struggling readers need some external reinforcement to get them started in reading, but if students are reading because of the reward, my guess is they will quit reading as soon as the reward is withdrawn.

I use two forms of reinforcement in SSR. The first is the grade, which is based on the Reading Records. Anyone who participates gets a good grade, and this is usually a sufficient reward for most students. The second reward is my comments and other students' reactions when we discuss their books one-on-one or in group book talks. Teens love to share ideas and hear one another's reactions to books, so this feedback reinforces reading. When students return to my class years later, I almost always hear a comment like, "I always appreciated it that you gave us the time to silent read in your class. That was one of my favorite things in all of high school." I've heard a variation of that remark hundreds of times over the years, stated with conviction. I truly believe that for most students, the freedom to read and the enjoyment of it are reward enough.

Q: Do you recommend using Accelerated Reader software or other computer-based programs to foster reading?

A: I'm in favor of anything that helps students improve their reading. However, I'm also in favor of keeping the SSR program as simple as possible. Adding computer-based quizzes requires access to both computers and software as well as time. I'd rather use the time for reading. Another concern is the point system used by the Accelerated Reader program. It assigns a value to each book; when students pass the quiz on that book, they receive a certain number of points. As I explain to my students every semester, I believe there is one true reason for reading a book: It is the right book for them at that time. The point system steers some students to books that will score more points, rather than books they truly want to read. In addition, a pretest assigns a range of books for each student. Some teachers and parents dislike this approach because students are not given credit for reading books that are above or below their assigned reading level. As an adult reader, I sometimes want to rack my brains over a book on theoretical physics, and at other times I want to get lost in an easy adventure novel. I want the freedom to choose, and students should have that freedom as well.

The point system also lends itself to formal and informal competition. Who can score the most points this quarter? In one incident, a school set up teams of readers who tallied points for their team. One team, which valued winning above reading for enjoyment, soon discovered that one team member could read a book and take the quiz for himself and all his teammates by using their passwords. Thus, each book the team read was credited four times, once for each member of the team. It was a way to advance in the competition, but did very little to foster lifelong reading in the participants. When the goal is reading for enjoyment, competition doesn't fit.

The cost of computer-based programs is a significant deterrent. I have yet to meet a school librarian who complained of a budget that was too large. Accelerated Reader programs or other software used in a school often comes out of the librarian's budget. Comprehensive computer programs often cost hundreds or thousands of dollars—money that could buy many new books for the library.

My final and biggest concern with computer-based reading programs is limitations on book choices. Even though Accelerated Reader software boasts 75,000 titles in its collection, it will not contain every book that students want to read, especially in the genres of biography and nonfiction. If my student wants to read about how to throw farther in shot put, I want him to read that book, because it could contain the information he needs to win and earn a scholarship for college. While 75,000 titles is an impressive number, it is far too small for my concept of sustained silent reading.

Q: If SSR is so good, why isn't it used in every classroom?

A: I firmly believe that the single most important element in the success of an SSR program is the attitude of the teacher. If a teacher believes SSR is a great program and conveys that attitude to the students, my bet is the program will be successful. On the other hand, if a teacher doesn't believe it works, she probably doesn't use it in her class. And she shouldn't. If silence is not enforced, students aren't monitored for participation, and teachers don't model good reading habits, the program is bound to fail.

Some teachers might not like SSR. They may believe it gives too much control to students or uses needed lecture time for reading time. They may fear having to justify SSR activities against curricular requirements. Or perhaps they believe that students should write book reports on everything they read. These reservations could create doubts about SSR and the class time it requires. Yet teachers who give SSR an honest chance see the amazing results it produces and often quickly change their opinion. It is wonderful to sit in a room with 25 teenagers deeply engaged in reading. For many teachers, that scene confirms the power of silent reading. You can see a glow in the eyes of teachers who believe in sustained silent reading.

Q: Instead of 10 minutes per day, couldn't I just save the time up and give 50 minutes of SSR every Friday?

A: You could. If this were math class, things would balance. After all, 50 minutes is 50 minutes. But SSR is not an equation, and in the world of SSR, 5 times 10 minutes does not equal 1 times 50 minutes. I have seen teachers try SSR this way; nearly all stopped the program in the first semester. While reading a full hour on Friday is better than no student-selected reading at all, too often, I believe, students translate reading only one day per week into "Friday free day." If SSR just happens on Friday, students quickly see it as the thing we do after we finish our "real" work. They see it as the thing we do at the end of the week when we are all tired and are just hanging on until the weekend. They see it as the least important activity instead of the most important activity. If the books they really want to read come at the end of the week, these books must be less important than the teacher-selected materials.

If SSR is one day per week, students invariably forget their books. Instead of missing a 10-minute session, the student and teacher scramble to fill 50 minutes. By reading only one day per week, students do not get used to having reading books with them, carrying them from class to class and home in the evening, and they don't develop the habit of sustained reading every day, one of the most important results of SSR. Because of the gift of class time, my students read five days per week; however, I know from conversations and surveys that many, even most, of them read six or seven days per week and often continue the habit on through the summer and after graduation.

No running coach would ask his runners to save up their mileage and run it all on one day. Regular training leads to fitness, and regular SSR leads to "reading fitness." Trelease said reading is a skill, and the study (cited in Chapter 1) by the International Association for the Evaluation of Educational Achievement amply supports providing daily silent reading.

Q: What do you do if a student repeatedly forgets to bring a book to class?

A: From the first day that students are required to have reading books, I address this. I walk around the room to see that each student has a book. If a student doesn't have one, I ask, "Will it be here tomorrow?" or "Where is it?" The first day or two, I'll offer a gentle reminder, but after that I become more stern. The program is based on every student reading every day. Usually, one or two reminders are plenty, but occasionally a student can't or won't remember to bring a book. Because the program is so simple—bring a book, read, get a good grade—I crack down hard on those who don't participate. It is easy to get an A, but it is also easy to get an F if you don't become part of the program. Using my point system, a student who forgets a book twice would lose a letter grade on the SSR score for the six-week term. I know this harshness seems at odds with the "reading for enjoyment" concept, but I stress repeatedly how important SSR is and how easy it is to get a good grade. I give out few penalties during a school year, because the program quickly becomes a cornerstone of the classroom.

Q: How do you help a student who says, "I hate to read"?

A: To me, this statement really means, "I haven't found the book I want to read yet." As soon as I hear or read that comment, I meet privately with the student. We sit after class or in the hallway and talk about personal interests. I can usually suggest a book or two. If I can't, I arrange for the student to talk with our librarians. Often, that attention is all it takes to get a student headed in the right direction. Sometimes it takes more.

For example, a senior boy wrote the following negative comment in an SSR survey: "I'm not a big fan of reading. I just get bored with it and it doesn't keep me interested so I find myself day after day staring around the room." By the time he wrote that comment,

I had already talked with him on two occasions. I hadn't reached him. The students had written their comments on Wednesday, but I didn't get a chance to read them until Friday. After class on Monday, he stayed. Our conversation went something like this:

"I see on your SSR survey that things still aren't going well for you with the reading. I want to talk about that again."

"Oh, don't worry, Mr. Gardiner. That was last week. Over the weekend I found a book about a musician, the rapper DMX. I'm already 240 pages into the book, and I love it."

End of that conversation, but not the end of the story. A week later, I attended a hockey game. Just after I walked in the door, I saw this same boy. As soon as he saw me, he came over.

"I finished the DMX book. It was almost 500 pages. That's the longest book I've ever read, and I read it in less than two weeks."

"Nice job. I'm glad you found the book and enjoyed it so much."

"I wanted to ask you if I could borrow that Lance Armstrong biography you told us about?"

"Sure. It's on my file cabinet at school. Get it from me tomorrow in class."

Not all progress with students in SSR programs will be that dramatic, but it does happen often enough. Anyone who has taught SSR has similar stories, moments that make months of teaching worthwhile.

For years I had known that "it only takes one book to change a student's life." Lately, I've heard the phrase "home run book" to describe the phenomenon. Whatever the term, it is an amazing thing to see in your classroom. Your relationship with that student is forever changed and that student's attitude changes too. For proof, ask any Good Adult Reader you meet to describe her own home-run book. She can do it easily, and she can add details about where she was when she read the book, who gave her the book, why she read it, and how it directly led to other books or ideas in her life. A home-run book is a huge gift to a student. Although lifelong reading might happen without SSR in the classroom, the chances of seeing this dramatic change in a student increase exponentially with SSR because student-centered book selection sets the stage so nicely. Remember, "It only takes one book." Giving students the chance to read several books may lead to the one that changes a life.

Q: Aren't high school students too old for SSR?

A: In his book, *The Read-Aloud Handbook,* Jim Trelease tackles a related question: "Aren't high school students too old to read aloud to?" Trelease maintains that they aren't too old, and I agree. On more than one occasion, I've started class by simply reading aloud. I didn't explain what I was doing or why, I just started reading. They may be 15 or 17 years old, but they quickly get quiet and listen, trying to understand what is going to happen next, just like youngsters in story hour. They aren't too old for reading aloud, and they aren't too old for SSR. Most students are grateful for the time. When I look at changes in modern society, I understand why. Students are often forced to choose one sport and participate in it year-round. If not playing a sport, they often work long hours at jobs, sometimes full time around school hours. In addition, family obligations and pressures from friends and a hundred other things seem more important than reading the next 20 pages in a book. High school students aren't too old for SSR; if anything, they are the ones who most need time to read.

Q: Why don't you allow newspapers and magazines during SSR?

A: It may seem a contradiction that half my school day is spent teaching journalism, yet I won't allow SSR students to read newspapers or magazines. The main reason is the idea of sustained reading. Many read the newspaper at home or at work, and I want to give them a place to read something longer and more involved. Having said that,

I have, in recent years, received the local newspaper through the Newspapers in Education program. I initially signed up so my journalism students would have models of professional journalism in the classroom. I receive a class set of the local newspaper every Wednesday. We use it to look at leads, headlines, captions, and news writing style. The past two years, I've also allowed my regular English classes to read newspapers on some Wednesdays. It makes a nice break and sometimes helps me find students who have a natural interest in journalism and recruit them for work on our school newspaper. The basis of SSR remains reading a book, but the newspaper serves as a special treat several Wednesdays during the year.

Q: Do you try to connect SSR with your regular curriculum work?

A: Yes. In my opinion, SSR is regular curriculum work. One of the best uses reinforces reading strategies we discuss in class or illustrates the elements of literature. The essence of SSR is enjoyment, so I don't apply much analysis. One interesting connection that I don't design is that students often use SSR to follow up on readings from the curriculum. For example, in the spring we read a book called *Until They Bring the Streetcars Back* by Stanley Gordon West, a Montana author. Our department speaker coordinator, Kris Keup, arranges annually for West to visit with our students in the school auditorium. After meeting West personally, more than a dozen of my students read *Finding Laura Buggs* and *Growing an Inch,* sequels to *Until They Bring the Streetcars Back.* All three books take place in Minneapolis-St. Paul in 1950 during West's senior year in high school. His issues touch high school students, making his books very popular. His novels circulate freely from one student to the next and are often written up on the Read It Forward Web site. Thus, students use SSR time to stay involved with an author they know and admire from their curriculum work.

Q: Will SSR work with classes that are affected by mainstreaming?

A: It works very well. It is an excellent activity for classes with a variety of reading abilities, because each student is given the same assignment and is allowed to interpret it individually. Group assignments from the textbook might leave some students struggling and falling behind, but SSR allows everyone in the room to work and progress independently.

Comments from Students, Teachers, and Administrators

The existence of an SSR program in a classroom or a school affects many people in the building. In this chapter, students, teachers, librarians, and administrators express their views on how SSR affects learning and attitudes toward reading. The comments reveal several common themes about SSR programs, and the variety of responses and personal experiences clearly shows the impact of silent reading from varying perspectives.

Students

How do students respond to SSR programs?

- "The main thing I enjoy about SSR is that it gives me a chance to choose a book for school myself. I am very independent, and [I] like that I have some say in school-related assignments."
—Sophomore girl

- "The 10 minutes of daily SSR become the peaceful eye in the storm of school work, worry, and responsibility."—Junior boy

- "I like having the silent reading program in this class. I *never* used to read, but this program has gotten me to read a lot more and has opened my eyes to the world of books."—Sophomore boy

- "SSR is a great program and other students and their teachers should try the SSR program. Reading is good for everyone."
—Senior girl

- "This is a great way to get students to explore new books. I was not an avid reader before this school year started, but this year I have read over 20 books. I am now constantly at the library looking for novels I am interested in."—Senior boy

- "I think this is the best program at our school because if we didn't have it, I would probably only read a book when it was assigned. This program has made me smarter and more interested in books rather than video games."—Sophomore boy

- "I've been in the SSR program for three years, since I was a sophomore. This program has made me a better-rounded person and has made me enjoy reading much more."—Senior girl

- "SSR is a privilege and an activity I cherish. During the course of the school year, reading becomes a neglected secondary activity due to hours of homework, my job, and family duties. The opportunity to catch up on my reading in school is one I would not like to sacrifice."—Junior boy

- "I think that the silent reading program should be introduced into every English class throughout America. You come to class and get 10–20 minutes to forget about the troubles and worries of your life and indulge in the life or story of your book. It is an escape route for me."—Sophomore boy

- "SSR gives me time when I don't have to think about school, friends, family, whatever. I just focus on a book and relax for 15 minutes. It's helped me rediscover my love for reading."
—Junior boy

- "SSR is awesome. It gives us a chance to just be out of our bodies and into an author's world."—Sophomore girl

- "I think SSR is pretty cool, because it gives students a time to just sit back and relax from all the pressure school gives you."
—Junior boy

- "SSR allows us, as enriched English students, to express ourselves through our reading, which I know we all love to do even in our free time. The books we read on a given day reflect our mood and often lead to discussions and book sharing."—Junior girl

- "Silent reading is a good way to expand and broaden our knowledge and reading skills. The one disadvantage is that with all the books I'm already reading it is hard to keep enjoyable reading separate from school reading. I confuse books, so when it comes to quiz time, it's rather difficult."—Junior girl

- "My reading style is to sit down over long periods of time and read large sections of a book. The short periods every day aren't the best option for me. I read about three hours every Sunday."
—Junior boy

- "I love SSR. It gives me a chance to escape the "blah" of school for 10 minutes. I am totally lost in my book, as though in a different place and time. Only at the end of the 10 minutes am I pulled back to reality. If I had my way, SSR would be a class in itself."
—Junior boy

- "Reading, in and of itself, is immensely important. I take this seriously and read for at least one hour every day."—Junior boy

- "Silent reading is a very good program because it develops our reading skills by letting us read independently in a book that we enjoy. Also, if we do not like the book, we can stop reading it and get a new one."—Sophomore boy

- "Most people don't read because they don't make time for it. SSR makes that time. If I were not given SSR, I probably wouldn't read at all. It gets me started and moving."—Junior boy

- "Make sure you don't schedule a vocabulary test or other quiz for right after SSR time. If that happens, there is no way I can relax and concentrate on my book. I spend the time worrying about the quiz or glancing at my notes to prepare for the quiz."—Junior boy

How does SSR affect students within the classroom?

- "It's a good way to have uninterrupted time for reading. At the beginning of class, I feel more alert and my critical thinking feels more focused."—Junior boy

- "SSR is a great way to collect yourself before class begins. It gives students a chance to center their minds for what comes next."—Junior boy

- "I think silent reading is great. I have this class first hour and it's an awesome way to start the day."—Senior boy

- "I love having SSR. Having English after lunch is difficult. The transition from a time where you're laughing with friends to a time where you're expected to work can be tough. SSR gives me a chance to get back into a thoughtful mood."—Junior girl

- "I enjoy reading so much more because of SSR. I have gained a new appreciation for literature, and I now pick up a book in my free time instead of watching TV. I never would've done this before." —Senior girl

- "I think I learned more in this class than I have in any other English class I have taken. I especially liked the silent reading be-cause it helps me relax and escape from reality. Every night before I go to bed, I read 15–20 pages. I used to hate reading, but now, it's starting to grow on me, and it helps me move on through life." —Senior girl

- "Reading is the foundation of an English class. You cannot learn grammar, spelling, etc., without being comfortable with the written word. You become comfortable with the written word by reading. I feel SSR is the most important part of our class, and I learn the most from it."—Sophomore girl

- "It has helped me tremendously. It has expanded my vocabulary. I am definitely a faster reader, and now, I think that maybe, I even like to read. What happened?"—Senior boy

- "I will continue to read for the rest of my life. In fact, I already signed up for a college program next year where I will, in a two-year period, read the great works of Western Civilization."—Senior boy

- "I'd try to make SSR part of more classes than just English. Maybe not every day, but I think we should have reading time more each week."—Junior girl

- "I started to actually enjoy reading since I could pick the types myself. I began reading on my own time, which I *never* do." —Sophomore girl

- "I liked the silent reading time because it got me back into reading. Before this class, I hadn't picked up a book unless it was required for the class. Now I'm reading like three different books right now." —Junior boy

- "This was more of an adult English class because we were able to choose what we wanted to read, making us like what we read." —Junior boy

- "I loved the silent reading program, but felt that we should have had at least a few more days to just read. It would sometimes be incredibly difficult to pry myself away from my book and then have to try and concentrate on another assignment."—Sophomore girl

- It's a good way to have uninterrupted time for reading. At the beginning of class, I feel more alert and my critical thinking feels more focused."—Junior boy

- "When I started junior high, I barely even picked up a book without it being required. With silent reading, I have now become very into my reading and have found it hard to sleep without having at least tried to read."—Sophomore girl

- "Since I was little, I've always read, so the silent reading was no far stretch for me. Unfortunately, as I've gotten older, I've begun to lose the time I used to have to read, so snagging even a few extra minutes at school is a major help. Getting a guaranteed opportunity to read is really great."—Junior girl

- "I used to hate reading before my senior year, and now, sometimes I can't wait until I have English again to read some more. I really enjoy reading now. I think you have a great deal of influence on that because you didn't force us to read, you let us make the decisions."—Senior boy

How does SSR affect students outside the classroom?

- "I even went out and bought books to read on my own so you know I'm enjoying reading now."—Senior boy

- "I read in my spare time now instead of watching TV."
—Senior girl

- "I try to read for 30 minutes every night before bed."
—Junior boy

- "Because of the silent reading program, I will make more time to read this summer and for the rest of my life."—Junior girl

- "I am a slow-paced reader, and SSR doesn't pressure me to keep up with others. I love how we get to choose our own books. That improved my attitude towards reading because it gives us freedom in choosing books rather than forcing us to read certain books. SSR needs to be a part of this class."—Junior boy

- "SSR has helped me because now I love to read. It doesn't matter if it's a novel or a few pages assigned from a science book, I'll always read it."—Sophomore boy

- "I hardly have time to read because I work six days a week. This gives me time to read. I usually end up reading before bed though, because I want to see what was going to happen since I read earlier in class."—Senior girl

- "I can't believe I read 24 books this year. I wouldn't have finished or even started that many without the silent reading program."—Senior girl

- "I think I read about an hour a week outside class. It depends on how many other books I am reading."—Junior girl

- "I read for about two hours every night."—Junior girl

- "Since I found my latest book, I have read every night at home before I go to bed. No other book that I've read has been that good, but that one is, and I enjoy reading it whenever possible."—Senior boy

- "I read my book outside of class every chance I get, and my fondness and appreciation for reading have skyrocketed."—Senior girl

- "I read my silent reading book probably as much as I can outside this class, during other periods, and at home before I go to bed. In the last couple of months, I've probably averaged one book every ten days."—Sophomore girl

- "I read about two or three times a week before I go to bed. I used to never read at home."—Sophomore boy

- "Before I go to bed, I read about 10–15 minutes in my book. It gives me something to dream about."—Sophomore girl

- "I read as often as I can. In fact, I always have a book in my backpack (which is practically an extension of my spine during the school year)."—Junior boy

- "I read a book every night before I go to bed to help me wind down. I read for about half an hour or until I wake up with drool on my book and face."—Sophomore girl

- "I read my silent reading book for about two hours every day outside of class. I read all sixth period study hall and for one hour before I go to bed."—Sophomore boy

How do students feel about 15 minutes of reading time per day?

- "I wish we had more time to read. I get very involved in the book and I really want to read more, but we have to quit."—Junior girl

- "Ten to 15 minutes is perfect because it allows us to read a good 10–20 pages and still allows time for the teacher to give her lesson and teach us for the day."—Sophomore girl

- "I love spending time reading every day. I typically don't want to stop reading at the end of the time."—Junior boy

- "I love the program. Being able to select our own reading material allows us to read what we're most interested in. With the absence of deadlines, we can read at our own pace." —Senior boy

What are the benefits for students using SSR programs?

- "I enjoy reading because it introduces me to all sorts of interesting people."—Junior girl

- "I feel smarter because I get to choose challenging books and get time to read them everyday."—Junior girl

- "I used to just read books that were assigned, and so I read slow. Now I read twice as fast because of so much practice." —Sophomore boy

- "Silent reading has helped me get better grades this semester because I am understanding my text in other classes."—Sophomore boy

- "The program has helped my literature skills. By reading material from a variety of authors, I have learned many different styles of writing."—Senior boy

- "I don't know if SSR has made me a better reader, but it has helped on the emotional side. I am able to stop and relax, to take a breath and regain my composure."—Junior girl

- "It has helped me as a reader because I've been so busy with work, sports, school, friends, etc. It gives me time to slow down. I've started reading more outside of school, too."—Junior girl

- "It has helped my reading speed . . . my standardized testing in the reading section has improved."—Junior girl

- "I think the program has helped me as a reader because it has made me a faster reader, made me understand what's going on while I'm reading, and also I think made me a smarter person by increasing my vocabulary."—Sophomore girl

- "SSR has made me a better reader. When I was in middle school, we didn't read much, but now, I read a book every month."—Junior boy

- "I never used to be able to read that well, and now I can because of SSR. When I have to stand up and read in front of my other classes now, I can read and not feel awkward."—Sophomore boy

- "I learned to love reading. I have benefited greatly from the program. I gained a better and wider vocabulary."—Senior girl

- "In this class I increased my reading speed and the ability to comprehend what I read. My papers have improved, too, with my spelling and grammar."—Senior boy

- "Reading is the best way to stay in practice with the English language. It enhances comprehension, vocabulary, and is an excellent source of entertainment."—Junior boy

- "Recently I have been infatuated with 'classic' titles. Not only am I enjoying reading such authors as Hugo, Cervantes, Wilde, Dostoevsky, Kafka, and above all, Tolstoy, but I feel I am expanding my own mind and giving greater perspective to my developing mind."—Junior boy

- "Being able to impress people with your vocabulary and well-readidness. Yeah, that's a word. I read it somewhere."—Senior boy

- "SSR has helped me a lot. I think I read with more speed since I started, and I also find new vocabulary words in the books." —Junior girl

- "Reading each day has helped me to gain background information on subjects that I don't know a lot about. Each book opens a new world, and each book brings a different insight to what I already know."—Junior girl

How has SSR affected student attitudes?

- "I love reading more this year than ever before. I will continue silent reading forever. It has become a very important part of my life." —Senior boy

- "I really like this program because it gives me time to be by myself in my own little world. I am able to, in a way, evaluate myself."—Sophomore girl

- "Now I don't read just because I have to. I read because I want to read and learn new things."—Senior boy

• "I will continue to read forever because it can broaden your mind and I enjoy it very much. Being able to lose myself in a book is the best part of SSR."—Junior girl

• "Silent reading has let me read as a hobby. Normally I don't choose to read unless I have to. SSR has made me want to keep reading the books that I am reading in class."—Senior girl

• "The SSR program has taught me to like to read more. Before SSR, I really didn't enjoy reading much. Now I try to read almost every chance I get. Now I enjoy reading to its fullest potential." —Senior girl

• "SSR makes me enjoy coming to class."—Junior girl

How does SSR help student writing?

• "SSR shows us different writing styles, which allows us to choose the one we like best."—Junior girl

• "I write a lot and a book that reads roughly the same way as I write automatically sparks my interest. Books I read also greatly influence my writing style."—Senior boy

How do students choose SSR books?

• "My mom and I both love to read, so our house is full of books and she sometimes recommends them to me, or I just look through them and pick out one I want to read."—Junior girl

• "I have my SSR book for constant in-school reading and my stay-at-home book for off-and-on reading."—Junior boy

• "The way I choose a book is first, books I have wanted to read in the past but never had time to, then books other people would recommend and books I have already read that I enjoyed the first time."—Senior girl

- "Every six months or so, my dad and I go to the bookstore and buy a TON of books. Generally, he has some suggestions. Also, I usually spend about two hours in the store and just sit on the floor and read the book descriptions or the first few pages until I find books that seem appealing."—Junior girl

- "When I am picking a book, sometimes I look around the room and see what other people are reading. Then I ask some of those kids that share the same interests as me what they thought of it."—Sophomore boy

- "I ask my dad for recommendations because he has read a lot of good books. I change a book if I am not looking forward to reading it in SSR."—Junior boy

- "I read anything by Kafka, Hesse, or Anthony Burgess. Other than that, I don't know how I pick a book. Sometimes I read psychology books like Freud."—Junior girl

- "Right now I'm reading a Xanth novel, by Piers Anthony. I love his style, his brilliance with his imagination, and his play on words amazes me, so I am reading the Xanth series."—Junior girl

- "I choose a book that I want to read because of the author. Stephen King is my favorite author, so I tend to read a lot of his writings. I also choose books due to recommendations by others. If I'm not into the book by 50 pages in, I tend to try to find another one."—Senior girl

- "I mostly read classics. Usually I choose them upon my mom's recommendation because she has read everything there is."—Junior boy

- "When I look for a book, I search for books that are about things that I have to deal with in my life. I look for books about people that are similar to me. I also read books that my friends or family have read and said that it was good."—Sophomore boy

- "I listened to a speaker, then I bought her book."—Senior girl

How do students decide to stop reading a book?

- "I stop reading when it gets to the point that it feels like a chore to read."—Junior girl

- "I abandon a book when it drags on and goes nowhere." —Junior girl

- "I know when to quit a book when I don't come into class and have a desire to read that book, when I can't sit down and become a part of the world I am reading about. I know that it is time to find a new book."—Senior girl

- "I usually chose a book based on recommendations from family, a friend, or possibly from a magazine. I quit books when I find my mind wandering while trying to read them and when I dread opening the front cover."—Junior girl

- "I ditch a book when I am disinterested and feel that I cannot gain any knowledge through the book."—Junior boy

Do students have negative reactions to SSR?

- "I don't like it. I've never really liked reading and I took this class to write, not to read."—Senior girl

- "I sometimes like SSR and I sometimes don't. When I find a good book that I actually like and enjoy, I love it, and even read at home, but when I have problems finding a good book, I don't really like it."—Senior boy

- "I'm not a big fan of reading. I just get bored with it and it doesn't keep me interested so I find myself day after day staring around the room, but there are times when I really read the whole time and sometimes I do feel it's a good program. I never read outside class."—Senior boy

Parents

What do parents say about SSR?

- "It appears the program has been extremely helpful for [student's name]. By starting the book in class, he gets interested in it and reads at home to find out what happens next. I commend the Sustained Silent Reading program."

- "He has always read the sports section of the newspaper. Now he's reading weekly periodicals. He'll actually sit down to read."

- "I think this is an excellent way to help teenagers take or make the time to read. I would like to see a 'recommended reading' list from other students by category—fantasy, horror, nonfiction, etc. Perhaps students would be more encouraged to check out a book they wouldn't normally be interested in if they know another peer enjoyed it. It might be another way of exposing the students to different authors, styles of writing, and topics." (See discussion of Read It Forward, Chapter 4.)

- "It's made him read, which we've always encouraged. Plus, we've discussed some of the books he's reading."

- "I love the SSR program. It has my son reading. How can I keep him reading in the summer?"

- "I would encourage students to read not only books but the newspaper, short stories, magazines, etc."

- "Encouraging and providing silent reading times during class is a great way to get those who don't read much a jump start to continue on the rest of their lives."

- "Reading helps expand a person's vocabulary and understanding. I am a big proponent of reading."

Teachers

Koby Murray

Koby Murray teaches five classes of freshmen at Billings Senior High School, classes filled with struggling readers. She began using SSR eight years ago with first and second graders. When she transferred to the high school level, she brought SSR with her.

Murray allows her students to choose their own books. She believes this helps them get involved in the program. "When students are assigned books, it is just an assignment. When they get to choose their own books, they begin asking questions, like 'Is this any good?' They want my opinion, an adult's opinion, on their selections. They see reading as something fun. When it is self-selected, they enjoy it more. It is not something they do just to get a grade on it. It is something they choose, something they like."

Murray has her students write a brief summary of what they read each day. "This lets me help them in using the reading strategies I'm trying to teach them in reading class," she said. She likes the combination of reading and writing and added, "The more they read, the better they write and the more they write, the better they read. From the beginning of the year to the end, I see a huge improvement in spelling. It is so hard to teach that directly, because there is too much variety in their skill levels."

Since her students are free to read any books they choose, Murray talks to them about their choices. "They often choose books based on what their parents or siblings read and I often see parents and siblings reading books after my students have finished them."

She finds her students often get very attached to the books they read during SSR, sometimes to the point that they are reluctant to finish a book and move on to another one. "Just today I was working with a student, and he was really struggling with moving on to the next book. I gave him a copy of *Saving Private Ryan.* It is a thick book, and I wasn't sure he would want to read that much, but he said, "Trust me, Mrs. Murray, I'm actually getting into this."

Murray is convinced that SSR is making a difference for her students. Her primary goal in working with students in her reading classes is to make them love reading, and she believes that SSR is the best road to that goal. "Whatever is second place in making them lifelong readers is a long ways back."

Terra Beth Jochems

"The hardest part for me is matching a book that is right for each student," said Terra Beth Jochems, who has used SSR in her reading classes for the past 14 years. "That is so important. If students in 4th grade are willing to take on a project like reading a lengthy book like Harry Potter, it shows you it is a matter of finding the right book. The topic is critical."

Jochems, who teaches all four grades at Billings, sees students who don't want to leave a book when they finish it:

> Struggling readers need books in a series or books that deal with very similar ideas or themes. They can't get outside of a genre or series without going through a difficult time adjusting to a new situation. The problem for the teacher is that we don't always have the next book right there on the shelf. Perhaps someone else is reading the second book in the series.

Jochems has a large classroom collection of books offering a wide variety of topics and reading levels. She believes the classroom collection is a must, because many of her students read below grade level. With her concern for matching students with the right book, this collection makes her work much easier, although even then, it isn't always a simple task. One girl in Jochem's class referred to herself as a very reluctant reader and chose a book that is a poignant portrayal of girls in gangs, as Jochems remembered:

> She tried to shock us by choosing to read aloud sections of the book which contained street language. When she was reading

these sections, she would defend her reading by saying, "But you have to understand this character." It wasn't the book I would have chosen for her, but it was the right book to motivate her. Now she is reading *Eragon,* a very long, very different book and is being successful with it.

Reading selections from books aloud and discussing books in class are Jochems' favorite way of accounting for student reading. "The format book reports really set struggling readers up for failure," she said. "Instead, we share every Friday. They can tell us about a character, read a passage from their books, tell about a thought or feeling they had while reading. There is no pressure on them. They can read what they want."

Since struggling readers may also find writing difficult, Jochems has discovered one way of helping them complete significant work but have options about how they are graded:

> In working with these struggling readers, I often grade them on the effort they put in. Sometimes one student may say, "I don't want to write that paper." I offer them a trade for additional reading. Maybe I'll let them read an adolescent book that I don't have time for and then tell the class what it is about. I'll trade that with them, and for some students, it is a very successful substitute.

Jochems surveyed her students to find out how many had faked reading in a classroom in the past. Most had. She asked how many had faked book reports. Most had. That's why the book discussions and readings are so successful for her. The students are sharing the parts of the books that mean the most to them and that personal involvement is critical to the process, Jochems said. "For many teens, peer pressure, home problems, and school issues dominate their lives. You know SSR is something powerful when it can get them past that and make them really excited about reading and doing something in school."

Jochems believes that the atmosphere in a classroom is very important:

Struggling readers often fail to learn to read for pleasure when sitting in a regular desk. They need something different, so I have a room with couches, lamps, plants and posters that give the room an ambience that says reading can be pleasurable. I read along with them every day. When the class is reading, the teacher must be reading. You can't hand out papers or do other work. When SSR doesn't work for teachers, it is because they are not readers themselves. They are forcing themselves to sit there, perhaps even doing some fake reading themselves and watching the clock. The kids know this right away and the modeling fails.

Like Murray, Jochems often uses SSR to reinforce classroom skills such as reading strategies. She also has students identify vocabulary words or complete exercises based on phonics or fluency based on their SSR books. "I use SSR to my advantage all the time," she said. "You can teach a lot of these things better using SSR than anything else."

In addition to SSR, her classes frequently read aloud. "Read aloud is the beginning of SSR. We often use choral reading, where I model fluency and expression. Struggling readers then have the protection of reading in a group rather than individually."

SSR helps Jochems monitor the quality of time in her classroom:

One of our math teachers figured if classes wait four or five minutes to get started while the teacher is taking roll, then pack up and huddle at the door for four or five more minutes, that can be as much as 15 hours of instruction time over the course of a semester. My students start reading right at the beginning, and sometimes I even use SSR at the end of the period.

According to Jochems, it would be "criminal" if schools allow students to graduate who haven't read a book, yet many students have done that in our society.

"SSR is the one thing that has helped them," she said. "I don't hear 'Mrs. Jochems, I don't want to read.' No one would say that to me now. It's not cool to not have a book."

One of her favorite sights is a classroom full of students reading:

> When they get involved in their books, it brings them peace, a sense of peace they may not feel in any other aspect of their lives. My heart breaks with joy when I watch a class of students reading. It happens to me every single time. I get tears in my eyes, and I'm getting tears in my eyes now just thinking about it. I wish there was some way to show teachers who don't use SSR just how wonderful it looks to see a class like that.

Nan Jones

Nan Jones came from a background filled with reading. Her father was a reading consultant, and she majored in English with a minor in reading when she was in college. No wonder, then, that she has used sustained silent reading in her classroom for the past 30 years.

When she taught middle school English, she had a classroom library, but with her shift to college prep reading classes at the high school, she now leaves students responsible for finding their own books. This works well for her students, and she said, "The kids pick books that are just right. The students level themselves."

Her college prep reading students are "college bound and can read, they just don't read very fast," she explained. "We do drills in speed-reading, and we do a lot of vocabulary by using analogies like they use on the SAT. To help them understand their reading speed, I have them count the number of pages they read in each session."

The time spent practicing reading is critical, according to Jones. "The eyes are a muscle and they need to be exercised. I let them use their finger to pace if that helps them. Often I have students come back from college and say, 'I have to read 10 books this semester.' They need the speed and comprehension."

With three decades of experience using SSR, Jones is a firm believer in its success. "SSR works with everybody," she said. "They are so happy. I always have several kids who won't put their SSR books away."

She has seen a direct connection between students' reading and writing. "As they use SSR more, their writing improves. I see more complex sentences, even with the basic classes. They can hear something from what they read."

Because her students "want some form of credit for their reading," she has her college prep students calculate the average number of pages they read each day. If the average is 21 or greater, they receive an A. If the average is 15, they receive a B, and if the average is 10, they receive a C. She also has students write a report comparing one of their SSR books to other books they read. "I let my English I and II students write extra credit book reviews on their SSR books. It is the only extra credit I give."

Jones said many students have signed up for her class knowing it is based on SSR. "SSR gives them an immediate structure," she said. "They come into class and they know exactly what they have to do. When we talk about books, they make comments like, 'You should read this one.' It is like a snowball as we go through this class."

Jones has had many successes with sustained silent reading, but one recent incident with a high school boy caught her attention. He stayed after class to tell her, "I'm saving my money to buy a book I want to read."

Kris Keup

Even though Kris Keup has been using SSR for 19 years in her high school English classes, she admitted, "I'm still learning about SSR."

Using SSR in the classroom seems natural to her because she grew up in a family of avid readers. "We had books and magazines everywhere," she explained. "We read a great deal and reading was valued. We discussed ideas around the dinner table daily, a family tradition."

Keup has developed several activities she likes to use with SSR. She begins the semester with a day in the library:

During the hour in the library, the librarians introduce the students to the space and give a few book talks. Then they help my students find books of interest. At the beginning of the period, I ask my students to discover at least 10 titles they might be interested in reading and list them, including title, author, and call number, and they turn the list in to me in the library that day. They may add to the list any time, and the list is kept with the book log in their individual class files. Any time that remains in the library may be used for SSR, in a pre-arranged "quiet area," such as our reference room.

On succeeding days, she expects her students to bring a book to class each day. If anyone forgets or has finished a book, she supplies a two-sided cart of books that students may browse, but they must make a selection before the class bell rings. She allows the student to borrow a book for the reading session. If the student likes the book, Keup sends him to the school library to check it out.

Each student in her class creates a reading log including spaces to record the title, author, call number, and brief notes about each book. Students keep these in their class files. Students may use these notes on the final test for one question, to write about one of the books read during SSR.

Keup has also created a mobile made of copper wire, formed in a spiral. As each student finishes a book, "he or she writes his/her name, the book title, and the author on a precut heart and attaches the heart to the mobile, which hangs as a visual reminder of SSR and of how many books we read."

Approximately three times each semester, Keup leads a book talk with her students. She begins by telling about a book she is reading, then students take turns talking about their books, sharing details about what happened in the book, what was learned, how the book was chosen, or how a character developed. Students then pass their books around the classroom so other students can see the books and gain ideas for future reading.

"It is so exciting to see the growth of student readers throughout the semester," she said. "SSR is a powerful tool to use in the classroom."

Librarians

Lyn McKinney and Jan Allen

Lyn McKinney and Jan Allen are the librarians at Billings Senior High School. Both are National Board Certified Teachers, and they have worked hard to make the school library an inviting, comfortable place for students and staff. They are strong supporters of sustained silent reading and are a valuable resource in helping students find the right books for the program. With an increased number of teachers using SSR during the past three years, McKinney and Allen have seen changes in the student use of the school library.

"I see a definite trend in an improved attitude of students toward reading," Allen said, adding:

> They are more interested in reading, and they see it not as a job or a chore but something they look forward to doing. Our circulation is definitely up, especially in the fiction section, and this is no doubt a result of the English teachers using SSR. Independent reading has really grown for us; that is, kids coming in on their own to get things to take home. Having teachers in the building using SSR is a good partnership for us. It is helping us.

McKinney said they are seeing students coming in on a more regular basis now:

> There were times in the library where the last time we saw a kid was the day he came in as a freshman and got his library card. Since we have more teachers using SSR, kids are coming in and saying, "I just finished reading this, and I really liked it. Do you have anything else like it?" We are seeing two changes in students when they are looking for books. The first is they are taking a lot more ownership in their book choices. Instead of them coming in and looking for the shortest books, they are saying things like, "I like this author" or "My dad does this so I'm going to read about it." They are making a stronger connection to books.
> One of the most exciting things for me has been the number of times we see kids come in here and say, "I have to get a book to read in Mr. Gardiner's class." They get a book and then the next time we see them, they often say, "Wow, that was good." Because they are

choosing their own books, they make connections to their own lives. It opens a whole new world for them. If all we do is let students read the books we require, they become totally turned off. They might plow through it, but they don't enjoy it until it means something to them.

Billings Senior High recently placed its entire card catalog on-line, connecting the school to 29 other schools and allowing the library to quickly find any resources students need. This allows students to find more of the books they want for SSR programs. This brings up another advantage McKinney sees in having students visiting the library more frequently:

One of our building goals is helping students become lifelong learners. By having them in the library so often, we can get them comfortable with the software we use, which is the same software the state university system uses. They will be at a big advantage when they are in college, not only as readers, but because they know how to use the tools to get the information they need.

However, increased library use has created one problem for McKinney:

We are stretched in here now. We have had to become better at reader advisory. Students are doing more reading and that has affected our purchasing. They give us so many more recommendations now, and we try our hardest to keep up with those. We really appreciate the students giving us requests, but it has become enough that we are planning a major physical change in the format of the library. We are out of room, and want to find a way to give our fiction section a wider space.

Having students in the library from the beginning of the semester has helped improve students' attitudes toward the library, according to McKinney:

When you bring your classes down to the library the first week of every semester, it really sets the tone. You show them that you respect us, and no matter what expectations they had about the library before, they see this is a valuable place. From the beginning, they get an idea of what we have to offer, and it takes off from there. As a result, we never have problems with your students. They know we are not mean people, and they know we will help them. It helps our relationship with the students.

Administrators

Scott Anderson, Principal

When Scott Anderson first started teaching high school English, he got the impression from teachers and professors that SSR

> was used for reading the text or reading assignments, getting students to read in a class but only within the curriculum. I remember having a discussion with a lady about SSR and she said, "Why would you take extra time to read something students want to read, because then you aren't going to have time to do the work you need to? Students should read outside class and then do book reports."

While Anderson understood the concern for covering curriculum materials, he admitted,

> I was curious about SSR and how that would affect students. I didn't think it was going to be that productive. I remember giving time to read the textbook and give book reports, forcing kids to read different genres. Kids would forget their books, and I would have to remind them, and it just didn't fit well. Then I met a teacher who used SSR and it worked. She told me you had to let them choose their own books. You don't want to just use the text, and you don't want to force them to read certain things. You want to get them to enjoy reading. She asked me philosophical questions, almost like Socrates, making me analyze what I was doing. She emphasized that students had to choose, because that was the only way to get them to read and enjoy what they were doing. As an English teacher, I loved reading, and that was what I did. I assumed that students would love reading, too. It really rocked me to the core to think about why we are doing things in the classroom, and I became more interested in analyzing that. I think that is when I became a much better teacher. I started to read and research more and take a more focused approach to what I was doing in the classroom.

Anderson's curiosity about SSR caused him to talk to several other administrators about the program. He said it was difficult to convince people that

> SSR is a quality thing. A lot of people, especially outside the English area, will look at this and say, "There's no way I'm going to allow students to sit and read in my classroom." I used to teach both English and history, and I always thought of them as the same. History is written and if you don't like to read, you probably don't like history. I remember battling with some of my colleagues in the history department about the importance of reading. I didn't necessarily call it SSR, but we talked about having students read some history books that they could choose on their own. I wanted to have them read the books for enjoyment and pursue some of the literature that goes along with history. There was a lot of hesitation. The attitude was, "I lecture about it, and they learn it, and I don't have time to be stepping aside and doing anything else."

Anderson recalled that when he was in high school, a teacher let him choose a book to read in class. The teacher didn't have a set time for silent reading, but allowed students who finished work early to read their chosen books. "I used to love that," Anderson said,

> and I brought my book religiously because I was so busy. I only had a little time to read, so instead of reading in the middle of the night, and being tired the next day, I always looked forward to getting my work done, so I could have that extra time to read. I've never forgotten that feeling.

Since becoming part of Billings Senior High School four years ago, Anderson has been more involved with SSR:

> This is the closest I've been to SSR during my career. I've been talking to teachers, because I have a personal interest as an English teacher as well as the building principal. I think SSR is a natural sponge activity. For example, when I look at the places I have evaluated, and I see what happens in the first 10 minutes of the class, the most productive classrooms are the ones where the kids come in knowing they are going to be engaged right away. That's something that I enjoy seeing. When I am in a classroom where SSR is going on, I see the kids come in and they transition from wherever they were before, wherever their minds were, wherever their bodies were. Their minds are in so many different places when they come into a classroom.

One is worried about her boyfriend and one is worried about getting beat up after school and one is worried about clothes, and with SSR, their minds are all working productively, efficiently and they are calmer and focused on something that is involved in the class.

As an administrator, I like to see kids come in and immediately become part of the learning environment a room creates. As soon as SSR is over, it is amazing to see how these kids are mindful and ready to continue and move on with things. It works much like Madeline Hunter's guideline for an anticipatory set. I have seen a difference in the kids and their reactions to their teachers when they have SSR in the classroom.

This reaction carries over when Anderson conducts teacher evaluations. "Most of the time when I go in to evaluate a teacher, I get some kind of a show," he said. "It's all about the teacher and what they want me to see about them. I actually spend more time watching the kids, because my concern is whether the kids are engaged and learning, not whether the teacher is performing."

Anderson also likes the modeling approach taken by most SSR teachers:

There is often a misconception about teaching in general that if the teacher is not in front visibly working, then learning is not happening. The idea behind SSR is that it is student-centered learning, not teacher-directed learning, and the idea of the teacher providing a model of a good reader is huge.

In thinking about effective use of SSR, Anderson has surveyed several teachers and observed students in classrooms. He believes that 10–15 minutes is the right amount of daily reading time:

Some kids really like reading and could go forever, but beyond 15 minutes seems to be too long for lots of kids and less than 10 minutes just isn't enough after kids get situated and involved in reading. From my experience, I can see when you have a few kids that are ADD and when they start fidgeting, they're done, and once they are done, the others are done, too.

Anderson also considered whether student attention spans could carry over from day to day:

I wondered if kids would get bored if they did SSR every day. I thought predictability would produce a negative feel for the students; however, I now realize that students come in knowing they will have SSR, while the other activities are different every day. I also realized that even the SSR part is not the same thing, because they are continually reading different books, different genres, so there is a change even within the SSR program. The topic is different, the excitement is different everyday, so they don't do exactly the same thing. It's not boring.

The recent No Child Left Behind (NCLB) legislation has left many school administrators scrambling for ways to improve student performance to meet the demands of the law. Anderson believes that sustained silent reading can be an important component in a program to improve student achievement:

Under NCLB, we are tested on our reading comprehension and our response to that reading . . . . Students have to be able to analyze and respond. In other words, they have to be active readers. If our kids are practicing for 15 minutes every day to be active readers, I don't see how that can't help. We all must use reading strategies to make sure that our students are engaging in the reading. Are they asking the questions they should? Are they organizing their thoughts? I think we need to be sure they learn those reading strategies and learn to apply them. If students know how to read, enjoy what they are reading, and know how to use what they read, then we are going to take them to the next level.

The success he has seen in SSR programs made Anderson dream of expanding silent reading to the rest of the school:

At one time, I hoped we could use SSR throughout the school, but the more I look at it in use and talk to teachers, I realize that having students use SSR every period during the day may not be that productive. To do a school-wide program, we need to do it in the right place, with the right environment, for the right amount of time. If you have too many chocolates, it's going to make you sick. The joy has to be there. The desire has to be there.

One of the biggest benefits of reading is confidence, according to Anderson:

I had a great professor in college. He forced us to read articles every day. We had to read and respond every day. We had to defend our argument every day. He put us in groups, and we had to come up with a consensus in a short amount of time. It was amazing how difficult it was for my classmates to become part of that because of their lack of confidence in their reading. I would be able to read and pull out things and others would say "How did you find that? I had trouble reading it." They hadn't practiced it, and they were going to be leaders in education. The ability to read and to get ideas from reading has been one of the best skills in the world for me. Look at my desk. I have to read pages and pages every day.

Research Regarding SSR

Lyman Hunt, the Vermont university professor credited with creating the concept of SSR (or as he called it, USSR, uninterrupted sustained silent reading), knew he had discovered something significant for teachers and students. He wrote,

> USSR is the essence of reading power, the ability to keep going with ideas in print. Without it the reader is crippled; with the power of sustained silent reading the reader is on his own, he can propel himself through print. He is an independent reader and does not depend on outside direction by the teacher. (1997, p. 278)

In the years that SSR has been in use, it has come under the scrutiny of literally hundreds of academic studies. The vast majority of these studies have found SSR an effective method of helping students learn needed skills. Block and Mangieri (2002) point out that

> during the past 25 years, several studies have demonstrated the benefits of providing more opportunities at school for students to read for pleasure and to develop their recreational, self-selected literacy habits. To illustrate, students who spent more time in recreational reading activities (a) scored higher on comprehension tests in grades 2, 4, 8, and 12; (b) had significantly higher grade-point averages; and (c) developed more sophisticated writing styles than peers who did not engage in recreational reading. (p. 572)

Characteristics of Successful SSR Programs

Many reasons exist for the success of SSR programs. One researcher, Janice Pilgreen, director of reading at the University of La Verne in California, examined a variety of sustained silent reading programs and found that successful programs shared common characteristics. In her book *The SSR Handbook: How to Organize and Manage a Sustained Silent Reading Program* (2000), she identified eight characteristics of successful SSR programs (Figure 6.1).

Pilgreen based her work on analysis of 32 free-reading studies containing 41 experimental groups. Each study measured at least two components, including improving student reading comprehension/achievement and increasing student motivation to read. Her analysis showed that 10 of these studies successfully attained statistically significant results in reading comprehension and that 7 attained such results in reading motivation. The remaining 15 attained

"observable" growth in reading motivation—that is, improvement which could be quantified but not interpreted through the use of inferential statistics. For each experimental group that reached statistical significance, a comparable control group operated; in the case of the groups that made only observable growth, there were no control groups. Interestingly, in the cases where the experimental groups did not do significantly better than the control groups, they did just as well, with the exception of two groups. And, in these two groups, where various combinations of SSR and skills were used, the amount of actual SSR time was not possible to calculate. Based on these results, I was able to conclude that SSR provided at least the same or better benefits for students in the areas of comprehension and motivation as traditional skills classes did. This is an astounding finding, particularly when we consider which alternative is more enjoyable for students. Clearly, free reading is less work than skill and drill and a good deal more fun. (2000, p. 5)

Cullinan (2000) also examined common traits of successful SSR programs and found that effective programs are essentially the same for primary, intermediate, middle school, and young adult students. In his manuscript, he cited "active parental involvement in student

Figure 6.1

Pilgreen's Eight Factors to a Successful SSR Program

1. Access: Students must have access to books from a classroom library, school library, or other source, but materials must be readily at hand.

2. Appeal: Reading materials should be interesting enough to make the students want to read them. Allowing students to choose their own books can take care of this.

3. Conducive environment: Students need a quiet, comfortable place to read.

4. Encouragement: Students need encouragement from teachers, parents, and/or peers to stay interested in reading until it becomes reward in itself.

5. Staff training: Pilgreen found that 60 percent of SSR programs are organized by teachers with no training in SSR. She believes training is an important part of establishing a successful SSR program.

6. Nonaccountability: "In order to get the most enjoyment possible from their reading, [students] should feel no obligation associated with it," Pilgreen states (p. 15). She found that 87 percent of successful SSR programs followed a rule of no accountability.

7. Follow-up activities: Activities—including role-play, discussion, book talks, and read alouds—should allow students to remain enthusiastic about a book without the feeling of accountability.

8. Distributed reading time: Most of the programs she studied offered students 15 to 30 minutes of reading time per session. More than half of them read daily, and 97 percent read at least twice a week. She learned that "making reading a habitual activity appeared to be a characteristic that differentiated the successful programs from the unsuccessful ones" (p. 18).

Source: Pilgreen, J. (2000). *The SSR handbook: How to organize and manage a sustained silent reading program.* Portsmouth, NH: Boynton/Cook Publishers, Inc.

learning, partnerships among community institutions, and collaboration among school and public librarians and teachers" as important factors. He found that

> the added freedom of middle school and young adult students makes it imperative to give adequate time for independent, self-chosen reading, to demonstrate the value and pleasure of reading and writing, and to make technology available in the search for information. (2000)

In *The Read-Aloud Handbook,* Jim Trelease calls SSR the "natural partner" of reading aloud. It was interesting to see how Trelease's view of SSR has developed over the years. I first read the 1984 edition of *The Read-Aloud Handbook* in the late '80s. I was already in favor of reading aloud, even to high school students, and Trelease confirmed my beliefs. In the 1984 edition, he devotes a five-page chapter to sustained silent reading. More recently, I reread his book, but this time I read the 2001 edition. The five-page chapter on SSR is now 36 pages; references to SSR permeate the remainder of the book. Trelease (2001, p. 3) believes a two-part formula explains why SSR works:

> • The more you read, the better you get at it; the better you get at it, the more you like it; and the more you like it, the more you do it.
> • The more you read, the more you know, and the more you know, the smarter you grow.

He noted that one important factor in SSR success, especially with low-ability readers, is that students be left alone to read, to concentrate, and to work, rather than be interrupted frequently to answer teachers' questions. He found that

> though poor readers are apt to be the biggest resisters to SSR, they also can be the biggest beneficiaries because of the profound differences between classes for good readers and those for low-level readers. Good readers read three times as many words per day, with 70 percent of their reading done silently, while the poor readers do their 70 percent orally. A study of 14 high- and low-achievement schools showed a negative correlation to the amount of oral reading but a

large positive connection to the amount of silent reading. Having to do large amounts of oral reading by poorer readers slows them down and widens the gap between themselves and better readers. This is only exacerbated when the teacher interrupts to make corrections, which happens more frequently with poor readers. SSR offers a welcome respite from the interruptions, assessments, and oral performances. Poor readers will be free to read a book for the purpose for which it was written—to be enjoyed and/or absorbed. (2001, p. 112)

Trelease is a fan of using SSR in the home. He asserts that because students, by the end of eighth grade, spend 95,000 hours outside of school and only 9,000 in school, parents could make a large difference for students by using SSR in the home. If parents set aside a regular amount of time, provide access to books, and serve as model adult readers, Trelease believes all the research on SSR in schools applies equally to the home.

While much of the research on SSR has occurred in the United States, several studies have been conducted on programs outside the country. Chow and Chou (2000) report that an SSR program was implemented in schools throughout Hong Kong and met with success. In an interesting study conducted by Aranha (1985), SSR was introduced to a school in Bombay, India. Aranha (p. 214) explains that Indian students "have traditionally been taught to read through rote methods, often with the result that many never develop good comprehension of what they read." Students in fourth grade were given SSR twice per week. They were tested before the program began, in July 1983, and then after, in March 1984. Aranha reports that the SSR group recorded a significant improvement in reading attitude during the treatment period and the control group showed a loss in attitude scores. In achievement, the SSR group demonstrated significant improvement, while the control group showed minimal improvement. Aranha also reports a gender variation: The girls in the SSR group showed a larger gain in reading achievement than did the boys.

The National Reading Panel Controversy

Not all research on SSR is positive. In 2000, the National Reading Panel (NRP) conducted a survey of reading research to determine what was working well in the nation's schools. In a section devoted specifically to independent silent reading, the NRP admitted that SSR has become a widely used technique for fostering reading, although it deemed the literature supporting its use to demonstrate "correlation" rather than "causation." It believed the studies simply point out that better readers read more often, but fail to show that the frequent reading causes them to be better readers. Using criteria that eliminated many of the positive reports on SSR, the NRP

> was unable to find a positive relationship between programs and instruction that encourage large amounts of independent reading and improvements in reading achievement, including fluency. In other words, even though encouraging students to read more is intuitively appealing, there is still not sufficient research evidence obtained from studies of high methodological quality to support the idea that such efforts reliably increase how much students read or that such programs result in improved reading skills. (2000)

While withholding support for SSR in American classrooms, the NRP did include a modest disclaimer:

> These findings do not negate the positive influence that independent silent reading may have on reading fluency, nor do the findings negate the possibility that wide independent reading significantly influences vocabulary development and reading comprehension. Rather, there are simply not sufficient data from well-designed studies capable of testing questions of causation to substantiate causal claims. (2000)

Several authors, including Krashen (2001), contend that the NRP failed to include several significant studies and excluded other studies that should have been part of their overall consideration. The NRP's failure to support SSR is in error, according to Krashen, who asserts that many more studies support SSR. He points out that "the addition of more studies to the analysis provides substantial evidence in support of the effectiveness of recreational reading." (Krashen, 2001, p. 121)

Writing in *Educational Leadership,* editor Marge Scherer (2004, p. 5) comments that the panel

> withholds its approval of sustained silent reading and other practices that the reading research studies it selected do not show to be significantly effective and generalizable for all students. This, however, does not mean that the other practices don't work in many classrooms— only that the research cited by the National Reading Panel does not prove they do.

Other problems face teachers who want to utilize the benefits of silent reading time. Block and Mangieri (2002, p. 572) surveyed elementary teachers regarding recreational reading in the classroom and discovered that the amount of time spent on SSR has decreased over the past two decades. They observe that "in response to the plethora of state-mandated, criterion-referenced high-stakes literacy tests, many teachers have been asked to spend more time teaching isolated skills and strategies." Tipaldi (2004) also notes that teachers are being squeezed for time because of mandated assessments and cautioned them to keep SSR as a valuable part of their classes.

Howard Gardner, creator of the multiple intelligences model, warns educators to find a balance between getting students ready for testing and giving them lifelong skills:

> Indeed, the pursuit of basic skills may sometimes be counterproductive. In the effort to make sure that students "cover" the curriculum and are prepared for various milestones and tests, teachers may inadvertently be undermining more crucial educational goals. At a conference I recently attended, an educator was defending a focus on the mimetic learning of concepts. She argues that by using such an approach "teachers can cut short the discovery process and save students time." In the current environment, it is understandable that teachers might feel the need to save time, but unless students come to appreciate why the skills and concepts are being inculcated and how to make use of them once they leave school, the entire classroom regimen risks being a waste of time. (1991, p. 187)

In looking at recent research on how students learn in the classroom, it is easy to see how SSR fits into current educational theories. Robert Marzano and colleagues (2001) assert that students learn new information by using linguistic and nonlinguistic modes. The linguistic mode is based on words—teachers and students talking, writing, and reading—and the nonlinguistic mode is based on images or mental pictures that students create in their minds as they learn new concepts. Marzano states that "studies have consistently shown that the primary way we present new knowledge to students is linguistic" (p. 73). If this is true, then SSR, as a means of working with language and practicing the linguistic mode, becomes more important because of the nature of today's classrooms and teaching practices.

One of the objections to SSR is that the teacher, while modeling the reading process, is not providing direct instruction. The opportunity to read is presented and students are left alone to make choices and to read. Students love this sense of freedom and control over their own educations, yet many educators worry about the lack of direct instruction. Krashen's complexity argument (discussed in Chapter 1) provides a basis for understanding why students are able to learn from silent reading on their own. His beliefs are supported, not only by Marzano but also by Howard Gardner, in his discussion of learnability theory:

> According to proponents of learnability theory, it would be impossible for any organism ever to be able to master the kinds of languages that all human beings master if that organism had to consider every conceivable set of rules that might govern that language. Indeed, the facts of the matter (say the theorists) are precisely the opposite. Human beings learn languages with ease precisely because, on the one hand, they come to the task equipped with powerful assumptions about what any natural language must be like, and on the other, they do not even consider the countless rival hypotheses about what might in fact obtain with all conceivable (but non-naturally occurring) languages. (1991, p. 59)

Children are able to learn languages even when they are not directly taught how to speak those languages. They are even able to learn languages when they are not instructed in what Gardner calls "negative evidence" or "evidence of impermissible utterances." He points out that

> children are not exposed to reliable information about impermissible utterances. Either this means that children cannot learn language (a fact we know to be empirically incorrect!) or it means that children must come equipped with various built-in assumptions about how to master the language that is spoken in their midst. On a learnability account, children learn to speak their native language even in the absence of negative evidence because particular assumptions about the nature of natural languages are part of their innate knowledge. (1991, p. 59)

Gardner continues, "The long list of possible errors that children never make and of unmodeled mistakes that they predictably make point to powerful constraining forces at work in children's language learning routines" (p. 61).

Aliteracy

Much of the research and commentary related to SSR deals with the rate of aliteracy among both students and adults. Aliterates can read and have the necessary skills to decode and comprehend a piece of writing, but they choose not to. Increasing student motivation, and thereby overcoming aliteracy, is a primary concern in much of the literature about SSR.

One powerful aspect of SSR in increasing reader motivation is self-selection of books. Critics of SSR contend that students will miss core curriculum if they choose their own books. I have yet to read a study on SSR that recommends throwing the standard curriculum out the window, using only SSR for teaching reading. The general belief among SSR advocates is that SSR is the strongest available supplement to the regular curriculum and is most effective as a balance to teacher-selected texts.

SSR allows students to make choices about what they read and when they read it. This choice is vital to the process of helping students become Good Adult Readers. Nancie Atwell, in her book *In the Middle,* explained that if educators want students to enjoy and appreciate literature, we must allow them to "exert ownership and choose the literature they will read" (1987, p. 161). Regarding her own growth as a reader, Atwell explains,

> I never read, in any genuine sense of the word, much of the literature on which I fixed any teenage eyes. I was in fact a good reader, but a different reader—a different person—than today. When I was ready for complicated and complex themes and language, those books were there waiting for me to enter and enjoy. That I did go back was in spite of, not because of, my own teachers' spoonfeeding and force-feeding. I chose to do so. Making the choice was my first step toward understanding and appreciating the literature. (p. 161)

Jim Trelease, in *The Read-Aloud Handbook,* defines the problem of aliteracy. "The scores tell us that many of our students know how to read, but their behavior as children and adults tells us they don't like it enough to do it very often. We've taught children how to read but forgotten to teach them to want to read" (2001, p. 5). He also suggests a solution to the problem:

> If the majority learn to read but don't read, we must ask: Why are they not reading? The only logical answers are either because they don't like it or because they don't have the time. There are no other major reasons. Eliminate those two factors and you've solved the American literacy dilemma. Reading aloud goes to work on the first factor, and SSR attacks the second. (p. 108)

In his book *The Unschooled Mind,* Howard Gardner further explains the problem of aliteracy:

> Beyond question, students ought to be literate and ought to revel in their literacy. Yet the essential emptiness of this goal is dramatized by the fact that young children in the United States are becoming literate in a literal sense; that is, they are mastering the rules of reading and writing, even as they are learning their addition and multiplication tables. What is missing are not the decoding skills, but two other facets: the capacity to read for understanding and the desire to read at all. Much the same story can be told for the remaining literacies;

it is not the mechanics of writing nor the algorithms for subtraction that are absent, but rather the knowledge about when to invoke these skills and the inclination to do so productively in one's own daily life. (1991, p. 187)

In Chapter 4, I briefly discussed one interesting phenomenon that frequently occurs during SSR: the "home run book." Usually a single book, or perhaps a series of books, changes a student's attitude from complacency to motivated reader. Von Sprecken, Kim, and Krashen (2000) in a study of 224 student readers found that 216, or 96 percent, reported that they enjoyed reading and 118, or 53 percent, could identify a particular book that created their interest in reading. Trelease found similar results:

In two studies built around the idea of "home run books," the majority of avid student readers could name favorite books that inspired them to keep reading, while those who disliked reading complained that it was "boring" and were unable to name a favorite book. Plainly, the bored readers haven't yet found the right book. This is still another reason to incorporate SSR across the grades. Just as you can't hit a home run if you're not in the lineup, you can't discover a "home run book" if you're not reading, or if no one thinks it's important enough to give you time to do it. (2001, p. 137)

It is clear that if we want students to read, want them to enjoy reading, and want them to become lifelong readers, we must give them both the freedom to choose some of the materials they read and the time to read and enjoy those materials. These two components are the essence of sustained silent reading and are critical steps in helping students become motivated to read throughout their lives.

Vocabulary and Spelling

Many studies have examined the effects of SSR programs on how students learn vocabulary. Strong evidence shows that SSR may be one of the most effective methods of increasing vocabulary. In fact, it is almost as if, in using SSR in the battle to overcome aliteracy, educators, as a side benefit, gain an incredibly effective tool for teaching vocabulary, spelling, comprehension, fluency, and reading rate.

The primary difficulty in teaching vocabulary is the sheer size of the job. Nagy and Anderson (1984) estimate that the English language contains about 88,500 distinct words. Teaching vocabulary to a typical student, then, is a daunting task, and Nagy and Anderson contend that even the most comprehensive direct instruction program available would fall far short of the job. They estimate that a vocabulary program that spends one-half hour per day on direct instruction and exposes students to a word 10–18 times during a variety of tasks could cover a range of 200–400 words per school year, depending on other variables within the program. Even though some critics say vocabulary cannot be successfully learned from chance encounters in independent reading, Nagy and Anderson (1984, p. 327) note that because of the above numbers, "Logic forces the conclusion that successful readers must learn large numbers of words from context, in most cases on the basis of only a few encounters."

Nagy and Anderson (1984, p. 327) hypothesize that the key to vocabulary learning is the "volume of experience with language." SSR programs are an excellent means of providing students with language experiences and give ample opportunities for students to learn words from context that are meaningful to them. Nagy and Anderson conclude that

> any program of direct vocabulary instruction ought to be conceived in full recognition that it can cover only a small fraction of the words that children need to know. Trying to expand children's vocabularies by teaching them words one by one, ten by ten, or even hundred by hundred would appear to be an exercise in futility. (p. 328)

In a later, related study, Nagy, Anderson, and Herman (1987) discovered that children between grades 3 and 12 learn words at the rate of about 3,000 per year. They write, "Children learn most new words incidentally from context while reading and, of course, while listening" (p. 238). Their research convinced them that the most effective way to help students increase their vocabulary was to get students to read frequently. "Our results demonstrate beyond reasonable doubt that incidental learning of word meanings does take place during normal reading" (p. 261).

One aspect of this learning that is significant for these researchers is the role of schema in learning new vocabulary. Nagy, Anderson, and Herman (1987) discovered that "the most important factor in learning from context is the degree to which the reader can integrate information in a passage into a coherent system consistent with his or her prior knowledge" (p. 264).

In studying 352 students in 3rd, 5th, and 7th grades, they found that students in all three grade levels "gained substantial knowledge about an unfamiliar word from a single exposure" (p. 266). They believe that multiple exposures are needed to learn all that is necessary about a word and its meanings, but they contend that "the results of this and our earlier studies indicate that wide, regular reading will itself provide the necessary exposures to words in a variety of meaningful contexts" (p. 266).

Trelease (2001) notes that the use of SSR as a powerful vocabulary-building tool can begin early in the student's career. "By third grade, SSR can be the student's most important vocabulary builder, more so than with basal textbooks or even daily oral language" (p. 111).

Because teaching vocabulary through word lists or other direct instruction methods often includes only a single definition or usage of a word, Krashen cautions,

> Vocabulary teaching methods typically focus on teaching simple synonyms, and thus give only part of the meaning of the word, and none of its social meanings or grammatical properties. Intensive methods that aim to give students a thorough knowledge of words are not nearly as efficient as reading in terms of words gained per minute. (1993, p. 15)

Through his research at the University of Wales, Ellis (1995) found strong indications that reading is a successful means of setting up vocabulary acquisition. He wrote,

> There is little doubt that naturalistic settings provide maximum opportunity for exposure and motivation. Reading provides an ideal environment for the implicit acquisition of orthography, and also, in individuals tutored in metacognitive and cognitive skills for inferring meanings from contexts, explicit acquisition of meanings. (p. 16)

One of the most interesting studies on vocabulary is referred to as the Clockwork Orange study (Saragi, Nation, & Meister, 1978). The researchers gave copies of *A Clockwork Orange* by Anthony Burgess to adult readers, who read the book knowing they would be asked questions about the content of the story. They didn't know they would be asked questions about vocabulary. The story contains 241 *nadsat* words, slang terms Burgess coined just for this book, defined in a glossary at the back of the text. The words have no meaning outside the book and are repeated an average of 15 times each in the book. The readers were given special copies of the book without a dictionary. The readers took the surprise vocabulary test and still scored between 50 percent and 96 percent (average score 76 percent) on words that could only have been learned from reading in context in the novel.

The powerful effects of learning vocabulary through independent reading are much the same for learning spelling by often seeing words in print. As Trelease (2001) points out, most people spell by visual memory, not by rules. As a teacher, I can't count the times I've been stumped when students have asked me how to spell a word. My first reaction, as it is for many adults, is to write the word down using several possible spellings and choose the one that looks right. Knowing which one is right isn't a matter of reciting memorized spelling rules to myself; it is a matter of having seen words on a page again and again until recognizing the correct spelling becomes instinctive. The more we read, the easier it becomes to recognize the correct spelling of a word.

While few researchers go as far as Nagy and Anderson in referring to traditional vocabulary and spelling lessons as an "exercise in futility," the wealth of research showing the positive effects of SSR on vocabulary and spelling acquisition must be considered by teachers and parents interested in improving student learning in those areas.

Reading Comprehension and Speed

The ability of students involved in SSR programs to comprehend reading materials has also been the subject of extensive research. Arthur (1995), in a study of 55 students in grades 4, 5, and 6, found that recreational readers scored higher on reading achievement test than nonrecreational readers. In surveying other studies, Arthur found that "children in kindergarten, primary and middle grades who have demonstrated a voluntary interest in books were not only rated to have better work habits, social and emotional development, but scored significantly higher on standardized reading tests" (p. 2).

In a study at Mitchell High School in Colorado Springs, Kornelly and Smith (1993) used the Nelson-Denny Reading Test to conduct pre- and post-test measurements of vocabulary and reading comprehension. Students in eight English classes participated in SSR. Three other classes served as the control group. Kornelly discovered that at the end of the 18-week semester, the control group had gained .5 grade level or one semester's growth, while the SSR group had gained 1.9 grade levels.

In a study of a high school in Georgia that used POWER (providing opportunities with everyday reading) sustained silent reading as an integral part of its language arts program, Weller and Weller (1999) found that 64 percent of the program's teachers reported that students' interest in reading had increased, and 53 percent reported that the students' reading skills improved as a result of the program.

Melton (1993) found that SSR for 10 minutes per day for a six-month period resulted in improvement in the experimental group for both reading words in context and comprehending reading material.

Several studies have also examined the effects of SSR on reading rate. Dwyer and West (1994) conducted a study of 76 college education majors involved in SSR for 15 minutes per day, five days per week, for five weeks. Results showed a "substantial increase" in reading rate over the five-week period. They suggest a strong linear relation emerged between the number of weeks participating in SSR and the resulting increase in reading rate.

If understanding reading material is a skill, it must be practiced to be improved. The studies of SSR programs show that reading experiences provide an important element in fostering reading comprehension and reading speed.

High-Stakes Testing

A central goal among most teachers using SSR programs is to increase students' enjoyment of reading. In the process, they hope to overcome the problem of aliteracy and improve vocabulary, spelling, comprehension, and speed. It only makes sense that if students (or adults) are not engaged in what they are reading, they will not choose to participate. While we can force students to read while they are in our control at school and endlessly test them on the reading material, that heavy-handed approach creates students who hate reading and abandon it as soon as they leave school. The student comments in Chapter 5 clearly demonstrate that SSR is one of the most effective means of fostering reading enjoyment. The number of students who write me notes every year about how their attitudes have changed, how they have discovered or rediscovered a love of reading, or how they feel the success of finishing a difficult or long book is a powerful testament to the benefits of sustained silent reading. We can create all sorts of programs to teach reading skills, but if we don't teach students (or allow them to discover) reading enjoyment, the skills will be temporary and meaningless.

In the current atmosphere of high-stakes testing of reading skills, many would cancel SSR in favor of "drill and grill" activities, hoping perhaps that the extra time spent on worksheets or word lists might make up for lack of enthusiasm on the part of students (and teachers) for the mandated examinations. If students aren't allowed to choose stories they enjoy, to immerse themselves in narrations that cause them to dream, to meet characters they want to know in person, or to experience any of the other joys of Good Adult Readers, how will they ever enjoy reading of any kind? How will they ever care enough to pay any attention to short pieces of technical writing on a mandated test? They won't; consequently, test scores will never be as high as they could be if students truly enjoyed their reading, felt that reading was important, and sat down to do the test in a positive frame of mind.

The U.S. Department of Education (2003) understands the essence of this vital attitude. In its *No Child Left Behind: A Parents Guide,* the authors wrote,

> Reading opens the door to learning about math, history, science, literature, geography and much more. Thus, young, capable readers can succeed in these subjects, take advantage of other opportunities (such as reading for pleasure) and develop confidence in their own abilities. On the other hand, those students who cannot read well are much more likely to drop out of school and be limited to low-paying jobs throughout their lives. Reading is undeniably critical to success in today's society. (p. 15)

While it is wonderful that the authors chose to mention reading for pleasure, they do so in a parenthetical afterthought. They relegate reading for pleasure to an "other opportunity" that can be done after students are "capable readers." They have this exactly backward. It is reading for pleasure that will make them capable readers, leading to success in math, history, science, literature, and geography, not the other way around. If reading is "critical to success in today's society," let's put it first where it belongs and use the benefits of SSR as a springboard to success in all areas of academic concern.

No Child Left Behind: A Parents Guide criticizes the use of untested methods in schools:

> For too many years, too many schools have experimented with lessons and materials that have proven to be ineffective—at the expense of their students. Under No Child Left Behind, federal support is targeted to those educational programs that have been demonstrated to be effective through rigorous scientific research. Reading First is such a program. Programs and practices grounded in scientifically based research are not fads or untested ideas; they have proven track records of success. By funding such programs, No Child Left Behind encourages their use, as opposed to the use of untried programs that may later turn out to be fads. (2003, p. 18)

Because reading for pleasure was singled out in the earlier reference, and because this citation refers directly to Reading First, I assume that SSR or reading for pleasure is being included in the programs considered untested or likely to be fads. First, SSR has been used extensively in American schools for four decades, hardly a fad, and will not disappear any time soon. Thousands of success stories abound regarding the progress students have made using silent reading as part of their language program. Second, a wealth of research about the positive effects of SSR exists, but the advocates of Reading First will never read it because Reading First was based on the work of the National Reading Panel (discussed above), which eliminated much of the positive research about SSR from their consideration.

The removal of that research is ironic because *No Child Left Behind: A Parents Guide* explains how an instructional program can be deemed valid:

> To say that an instructional program or practice is grounded in scientifically based research means there is reliable evidence that the program or practice works. For example, to obtain reliable evidence about a reading strategy or instructional practice, an experimental study may be done that involves using an experimental/control group design to see if the method is effective in teaching children to read. (p. 18)

As the first half of this chapter clearly shows, there is extensive research based on scientific studies illustrating the success of SSR. The creators of Reading First based their work on five skills identified as essential by the National Reading Panel:

- phonemic awareness
- phonics
- fluency
- vocabulary
- comprehension

These five skills are effectively promoted by sustained silent reading programs. Given the complexity of language skills instruction discussed earlier in this chapter, using Reading First or any other single program to teach these five skills is limiting in many ways. Reading First may be part of a language skills program, but without an extensive program of student-selected free reading, students will not learn the application of these skills and will likely miss out on the greatest gift a school can give students—a deep, personal love of reading.

The National Assessment of Educational Progress publishes lengthy reports such as *The Nation's Report Card: Writing 2002* and *The Nation's Report Card: Reading 2002*. Both of these reports are in excess of 200 pages and carefully document a number of test exercises given to students to determine success in reading and writing. While these tests may be important in some sort of statistical sense, serious problems result from placing too much value on statistics that show how students were able to fare on specific tasks designed for the testing situation. If we are truly in the business of teaching students to read, to enjoy literature, to make reading a part of their daily lives, and to become Good Adult Readers, they need more skills than can be tested by these limited tasks.

The human side of education is buried beneath a pile of charts and numbers. Nowhere in the documents are students asked about their attitudes toward reading and writing. Nowhere are they allowed to make any choices regarding reading or writing. In short, nowhere in these tests are they allowed to be independent thinkers capable of understanding and expressing what they need and want to further their own educations. High-stakes testing may be a part of our educational lives now, but we must remember to balance those exercises with student-centered reading. Let them learn to love reading and choose to make it a part of their lives.

Lifelong Reading

One of the most important results of reading for enjoyment is the creation of lifelong readers. Feedback from students year after year supports the extent to which SSR instills a sense of being a reader, of being involved in reading for life. This process happens repeatedly in SSR programs and, for me, has become a normal and expected part of teaching with SSR.

Cullinan realizes how this process unfolds for students:

> They often choose light reading for independent reading because they enjoy it, and they become more fluent readers in the process. Adults who encourage students to develop the reading habit through light reading can lead them to further reading. Students must take the first step of developing reading fluency before they can take the second step of becoming avid readers. (2000)

Becoming an avid reader is a wonderful experience for students. They are excited to discover success in an area that for many of them had been difficult or confusing. The decision to read independently is important, but as McKenna, Kear, and Ellsworth (1995, p. 939) explain, "Because reading is an ongoing process rather than a discrete act, the initial decision to read becomes a decision to continue reading once the process begins."

At that point, students make the conscious decision to identify themselves as readers, a new way of looking at themselves that affects all aspects of their school lives.

Nell (1988), writing at the University of South Africa, noted that inspiring students to participate in spontaneous pleasure reading, or ludic reading, is the ultimate goal of any reading program. In his analysis of why readers choose ludic reading, he wrote, "The reader's reinforcements are to be found not in the words and phrases of the book, but in the cognitive events that result from the interaction between book and reader"(p. 8).

Nell explains that in media such as television or radio, the pace of the presentation is under the control of the producer, not the user, but "the pace of leisure reading is under sole control of the reader." He continues, "Readers' subjective reports indicate that they greatly prize their control of reading pace" (p. 16).

According to Cullinan, once the enjoyment of reading is in place, teachers can take readers much farther in their development. Through book talks, class discussions, individual conferences, or writings, students can be challenged to read increasingly difficult works.

Tovani (2000) emphasizes the importance of students' learning to work their way through difficult texts they may have abandoned earlier in their development as readers:

> I realized long ago that most struggling readers weren't going to love reading enough to choose it as a leisurely pastime. However, electing to quit when text becomes difficult is a choice that could have serious consequences. In a few short years, these students will be on their own. They will have to read apartment leases, car-loan contracts, income tax forms and material associated with their jobs. It's one thing to quit reading a chapter out of a textbook and fail a test. It's quite a different matter to quit reading an income tax form and miss out on a refund. (p. 49)

Becoming a lifelong reader is often a matter of making choices. "As they grow older and more leisure options are open to them, the prospect of reading will be weighed against available alternatives, each of which is associated with an attitude" (McKenna, Kear, & Ellsworth, 1995, p. 939). If reading has been associated with an attitude of enjoyment and is seen as a worthwhile activity, it will be higher on a student's list of options.

The benefits of making choices about reading follow students throughout their education. Valeri-Gold (1995) had her college developmental reading classes participate in SSR for 10 weeks. She discovered that SSR is effective with college-age students. She reports that her students increased their interest in reading, improved their attitudes toward it, and became active participants in their own learning processes.

Gaining a positive attitude about reading and education is key for students to become lifelong readers. Students who become lifelong readers are more involved, more aware, and more creative in their approaches to life. People who can enjoy reading and other flow activities are destined to be happier and more productive, explains Csikszentmihalyi:

> Such individuals lead vigorous lives, are open to a variety of experiences, keep on learning until the day they die, and have strong ties and commitments to other people and to the environment in which they live. They enjoy whatever they do, even if tedious or difficult; they are hardly ever bored, and they can take in stride anything that comes their way. Perhaps their greatest strength is that they are in control of their lives. (1991, p. 10)

Giving students control of what they read is one step in making them lifelong readers and lifelong learners and a major stride toward helping them take control of their lives. Making significant parts of the educational process student-centered is an important concept. As Gardner (1991) explains,

> Education that takes seriously the ideas and intuitions of the young child is far more likely to achieve success than education that ignores these views, either considering them to be unimportant or assuming that they will disappear on their own. The ideas of the young child—the youthful theorist—are powerful and are likely to remain alive throughout life. Only if these ideas are taken seriously, engaged, and eventually trimmed or transformed so that more developed and comprehensive conceptions can come to the fore—only then does an education for understanding become possible.
> Assuming that they take into consideration the young mind and treat it with the respect that it merits, educators possess concepts, materials, and techniques that can engender far greater degrees of understanding across the full range of students and the full spectrum of disciplinary topics. It is not easy to effect such an educational revolution; there will be setbacks, and certain kinds of misconceptions, rigidities, and biases may prove particularly difficult to dislodge. Development cannot occur in a day, or even in a year. But we cannot fall back on the assertion that these understandings are impossible to

achieve, nor on the faith that they will come about strictly on their own. Good teachers, good materials, and the right educational atmosphere can make an enormous difference. (p. 248)

Modeling

Several researchers have stressed the importance of the teacher's role in SSR. Cris Tovani (2000) believes that during SSR, teachers should model not only reading but also the thinking that readers use during the reading process. She writes,

> Mental modeling is an even better way to help students understand how good readers comprehend text. When teachers make invisible mental processes visible, they arm young readers with powerful weapons. Good readers engage in mental processes before, during, and after they read in order to comprehend text. I stop often to think out loud for my students. I describe what is going on in my mind as I read. When I get stuck, I demonstrate out loud the comprehension strategies I use to construct meaning. (p. 27)

Howard Gardner (1991) explains that the practice of teachers modeling the reading and writing behaviors they expect from their students has been a significant development in modern teaching methods:

> I believe that this small-scale pedagogical revolution has occurred because teachers themselves have discovered (or rediscovered) not only that they can write but that they actually like to write. This spirit is of course infectious, and children are soon drawn into the excitement about letters, words, and meanings. Similar effects are at work in reading. Children read not because they are told—let alone ordered!—to read, but because they see adults around them reading, enjoying their reading, and using that reading productively for their own purposes, ranging from assembling a piece of apparatus to laughing at a tall tale. Fundamental experiences that may in earlier times have been restricted to children reared in highly literate households are now made available to all the youngsters in the school. (p. 211)

By getting directly involved in the reading/writing that they expect from their students, teachers can create an atmosphere primed for learning. Gardner (1991, p. 242) asserts that it "is difficult to set up a literate culture unless teachers embody compatible beliefs and practices in their daily lives. Arts and humanities teachers have the potential to be practitioners and to maintain their own process-folios in a meaningful way."

McCracken and McCracken (1978, p. 406) examined many SSR programs and concluded that "all adults in the classroom have to read or SSR does not work." They tell two stories that clearly illustrate the power of modeling in the SSR classroom. In one classroom, the teacher stopped reading to look up a word in the dictionary. Before long, students were stopping to look up words as well. Another teacher watched his classes as they were reading and noticed that because he had been scratching his head while he was reading, several students were also scratching. When he stopped, they stopped.

According to McCracken and McCracken (1978), teachers send a series of seven important messages to their students by modeling SSR:

1. Reading books is important.
2. Reading is something anyone can do.
3. Reading is communicating with an author.
4. Children are capable of sustained thought.
5. Books are meant to be read in large sections.
6. The teacher believes that the pupils are comprehending (because he or she doesn't bother to check).
7. The teacher trusts the children to decide when something is well written, when something important has been read (because the teacher expects pupils to share after SSR). (p. 408)

When teachers read and discuss books with their students, significant changes take place in the classroom and in the lives of those students. Based on their observations of modeling, McCracken and McCracken (1978, p. 407) conclude that "what a teacher does during and after silent reading defines silent reading for children."

Part III

Where Do We Go from Here?

7

Connecting Reading and Writing

Several years ago, I attended my first writers' workshop. I had attended other workshops designed for English teachers to help them teach writing, but this was the first time I'd gone to a workshop for writers who hoped to publish their work (and make money doing it). It was a wonderfully eclectic group that gathered for a weekend of talking about writing and publishing.

I attended sessions on how to submit query letters, how to find markets for writing, how to deal with rejection, and how to organize a writing life. During breaks, I talked to writers who were doing every job imaginable to support themselves while they were writing. They were full of ideas and dreams; their energy was refreshing.

By the end of the weekend, I could see two clear themes emerging. Writers love to write, and they practice it continually. Writers love to read, and they read even more often than they write. Speaker after speaker referred to things they had read recently, readings that had changed their writing style, readings that influenced the direction they were taking and gave them new ideas. One speaker summed up the attitude by saying, "I learned to write by reading and reading and reading some more. If you want to be a writer, you've got to see what other writers are doing."

The writers at the workshop truly loved what they were doing, even if they weren't cashing giant paychecks for their work. They were writing because they loved the process, cared about their ideas, and wanted to be involved in the writing world. The enthusiasm I saw at the conference was exactly what I wanted to instill in my students, and I wondered how to do that.

When I thought about the comments made regarding reading, the connection became clear. The writers at the workshop were already Good Adult Readers. They were independent readers of the highest order and had taken their love of reading and carried it to their writing. I knew students could do the same.

What I heard at the writing conference showed me that writers valued the same things that readers do. They loved their writing because it was their own. They controlled the genre, the topic, the style, the pace, the entire process. The general principles of SSR were exactly what appealed to them, both in their reading and writing. I decided to look for ways to treat my student writers more like I treated them as readers. I've since found that other teachers—including Pyle (1990), who created a program called SSRW, or sustained silent reading and writing—have also seen the direct connection and modeled their writing programs after SSR.

As with reading, the key seemed to be to offer more student control of topics and writing styles. Students often tell me that their SSR books influence the way they write their essays or short stories, so I knew the carryover existed. However, giving students ownership as writers is in some ways more problematic than giving them ownership as readers.

A very good example came to me through a student who had been in my class as a sophomore. He had written some very creative pieces in my class, and I always looked forward to seeing his work. One day during his senior year, he brought a paper to my classroom and asked me to look at it. I took the paper and could quickly see his concern. It was covered in gallons of red ink. His teacher had actually written more on the paper than he had. He was a strong verbal student, a state champion on the speech team, and he was devastated. We talked about what he had written and what the teacher had written, but I could see he felt defeated. He had lost ownership of the paper. If he rewrote the paper to suit the comments, it would be the teacher's paper.

We discussed his paper at length, and he decided to rewrite it as requested. I assured him that every writer has times when he must write to an audience not of his choosing, but that he would have other opportunities to be creative and demonstrate his writing skills. I'm sure the teacher felt that she was just being diligent, but the heavy-handed sense of control left the student with no room for expression. As he rewrote that paper, his only focus was on meeting the expectations of his teacher, not on saying something meaningful or creating an original piece of writing.

Students need a teacher's help to become better writers, but they don't need a teacher's control. Many teachers constantly struggle with how much to mark on a student's paper to send him in the right direction without destroying his confidence. It requires teachers to walk a sensitive line, one that may be different for each writer. This is where knowing each student as an individual reader and writer can be invaluable. Teachers should also remember that every writer needs a sounding board for ideas and a second pair of eyes to look over a draft. That's where the teacher can help the most.

Another difficult balance for a teacher is caused by curriculum demands that require specific types of writing assignments during a semester. Again, I think the SSR program can be the model. Just as I teach the curriculum readings and use SSR to support them, I can support and balance the papers required by the curriculum with writings chosen by the students. I have found that students write more and enjoy it more if they get the freedom to choose topics and styles on at least some of their assignments. SSR also provides a time for thinking, allowing students to imagine a world outside of their own and to create and understand new ideas. All this is necessary for quality writing.

The connection of writing to SSR doesn't end there. Krashen (2001) examined several studies and determined that when it comes to writing, quality is not directly related to quantity. While students need to practice their writing, he found the most influential factor for improving writing was the quantity of reading done by students. "Hypothesizing that writing style comes from reading, not from writing, is consistent with what is known about language acquisition: Language acquisition comes from input, not output, from comprehension, not production" (p. 25).

Pulitzer Prize–winning author Donald Murray (1987) also recognized the important connection between reading and writing:

> By reading you will hear other voices that make language dance in ways you never thought possible. And this may help you hear voices within your own head you never heard before. By reading you will see subject matter you never thought had value made significant by another writer, and you'll see in your own world things that need to be written. By writing you will see how other writers make the ordinary extraordinary, switch the point of view from which you usually look at the world, turn the world inside out before your eyes, put you in places you did not know exist, give you ideas you never thought of, place you inside the skin of other people. (p. 247)

He continues, "Reading, always an extending experience, is even more so for the writer, who begins to understand through his or her own writing how reading can be made."

Modeling Writing

One further connection to SSR is the concept of teacher modeling. In the same way teachers model sustained silent reading, they can improve their students' writing by providing a writing role model. If students see teachers involved in the natural progression from reading to writing, as promoted by the speaker at the writers' convention and researchers like Krashen, Murray, and Trelease, they are more likely to make that progression on their own.

Earlier I talked about the idea of the home-run book. Student writers can have similar experiences.

When I was a junior in college, I looked forward to graduating and starting my teaching career. I wanted to be an English teacher, but I had no desire to be a writer. I enrolled in Advanced Composition, which offered a mix of poetry, fiction, essays, and responses to literature, and I had been enjoying the work. One day, I walked into the classroom and found that the professor had rearranged the desks. The students' desks were pushed farther back, and she was seated behind a long table covered in magazines. Throughout the course of her lecture, she opened the magazines, each containing an article she had written. She explained what the article was about and the process she had gone through to publish it. She never said we should try to publish our writing in magazines, but by the time I left class that day, I knew I would try to publish someday. She had modeled perfectly, and the effect of that day's talk has never left me.

After I started teaching, I helped a group of students set up a peer tutoring program. It was a great idea, and the students were enthusiastic about it. I decided to call the local newspaper to get them some publicity for their efforts. As I was walking to the office to use the phone, it occurred to me that I should write the article myself. I got on the phone and asked for an editor. I explained to him what I wanted to do and asked if he would look at the article if I wrote it. He agreed.

A few days later, I dropped off the article. He published it and asked if I had any other ideas. Over the next few months, I wrote other articles, and the next year, the editor offered me a chance to write a weekly outdoor sports column. I sent manuscripts to magazines and began a collection of my own published articles. Eventually, I published three books.

I have copies of these magazines and books in a file cabinet in my classroom. Every spring, after several months of reading, writing, and talking about reading and writing, I take a day to show students my magazines and books. We talk about how to get ideas, how to contact editors, and how to write articles. Someone always asks, "Do you get paid?" I tell them about the range of payment I've received for my writing. It is always a lively day and questions often carry over for several subsequent classes.

One of my best examples is a short piece I published in *Chicken Soup for the Traveler's Soul*. Because my students are all familiar with the Chicken Soup series, they are surprised to find that somebody they know has a chapter in one of the books. The ideas in that chapter are important to me. It's called "We Almost Did That" and is based on leaving the country to teach in Peru. Several people my wife and I talked to before we moved commented that they "almost" took an overseas job or "almost" left home to travel. I decided I would never say that. Because the chapter has significant meaning in my life, it is easy to discuss purpose with my students, and it sets up plenty of discussion about how to find publishing opportunities.

Many English teachers have not published articles and don't believe that it is their job to do so. Perhaps it is not, but even attempting to publish will change two things—how you view yourself as a writing teacher and how your students view you as a writing teacher.

If you haven't published an article, please try. It will give you a chance to examine your writing, to feel fear and doubt, to worry about what you write, to experience the struggle of writing. It is also a chance to feel the hope that comes with submitting it and the anticipation of waiting for the response. These are the things our students experience. If we only rely on our memory of writing papers as students, we can't identify closely enough with their efforts. More important, we are not modeling, because they can't see our efforts from years past.

Where would you send your article or poem or short story? Start small. Look around your community. Most clubs have newsletters. Your school district might have a community report card. Your local newspaper might have an education page or a hobbies page. Write a letter to the editor. It doesn't matter what you write or where you decide to send it. The experience of being a writer is important; that is what you will share with your students.

If you get published, you can have the joy of publication and the added joy of seeing your students' faces when you show them your work. If you get rejected, you have learned another valuable lesson as a writer and one that may do you even more good as you work with students. I have a file of rejection letters several inches thick, and I show that pile to my classes as well. They need to see what the reality of writing is—and we have fun reading my rejection letters aloud in class.

Some teachers may say they don't have time to try writing articles because they need to spend time on grades or with their family. Start with short pieces (which also have a better chance of getting published in most newspapers or magazines) and write once a month or once a semester. It doesn't matter how often, but do give it a try.

In addition to changing the way you see yourself as a teacher of writing, it will change how your students see you. When they know that you face the same challenges, they will ask you much more interesting and thoughtful questions. You become their ally in their efforts to express themselves, rather than the singular audience they must please to get a grade. When they see you in that light, it changes everything about the classroom. Heather, a sophomore, wrote me this note, "I like how you can help us with our writing, because you are a writer yourself."

Connecting Reading and Writing

Teacher modeling sets up the connection between sustained silent reading and writing, but the books themselves expand that connection. By participating in SSR, students immerse themselves every day in the world of writing. They see how published writers develop character, handle dialogue, create drama, build conflict, explain ideas, punctuate sentences, choose verbs, and address a host of other skills necessary for successful writing. These writers become excellent models for students, and students, both consciously and unconsciously, frequently use the writing in their SSR books as models for their own writing in class.

Ian, a senior on my cross-country team, was also in my English class. He wanted to read a book about running, so I loaned him my copy of *Running with the Buffaloes* by Chris Lear, an account of a full season following the Colorado Buffaloes cross-country team through their practices and meets on their way to a national championship. After Ian read the book, he immediately started his next writing project—an account of our own season from the first day of practice to winning a third-place trophy at state. It was a perfect project for him, because the book affected him personally, inspired him to write, and gave him an account of his senior season that will be priceless in the future.

Another senior, John, had just finished a Hemingway book and stated, "I don't know why this is, but after I finished that book, I can only write simple, declarative sentences." He worked this way for a couple of months until he read a Faulkner book (yes, both of these were his choices through SSR) and said, "Now, it seems like all I can write are long, complicated sentences that ramble on forever."

I've seen hundreds of examples of this. What students read in SSR directly and immediately influences their writing and their patterns of thinking. Not every book will change them forever, but the books they like and become deeply involved with will affect the ways they put words together, how they interpret and construct meanings, and how they express their ideas. Like the speaker I heard at the writers' conference or the basis of Krashen's complexity argument (explained in Chapter 1), SSR is how we learn language arts skills and how we learn to write.

Creating the Masterpiece

I wanted to use the natural sense of development from sustained silent reading to help my students. I looked for a direct connection between SSR and writing, a way of taking the concepts I've developed over the years for student reading and applying them as directly as possible to student writing.

For 10 years I taught school yearbook and newspaper classes in Jackson, Wyoming. When I moved to Montana, I left journalism behind and taught English classes for seven years. Then I resumed working with the newspaper and yearbook. Other than major advances in digital photography and computer technology, the yearbook format was similar to that of Jackson Hole. The newspaper class, however, opened a new world.

We wanted to give students the opportunity to take the newspaper class for English credit. Objections to this idea are many, including the use of English class time to sell ads, design pages, and construct electronic layouts. Photography and darkroom time used to be a complaint as well, but digital photography has nearly removed that concern. In order to keep the class oriented toward English skills and curriculum, I designed it to meet every English core curriculum requirement while still producing our newspaper, the *Bronc Express*.

I, of course, started the class with SSR. Students who carried over from the previous program were shocked to learn they would have to read every day in newspaper class, even though they would benefit more than most students because of the amount of required writing. This worked well because the reading requirement for the composition classes (where the emphasis is on writing, not reading) stated "teacher-selected literature." Because the curriculum left the literature choice to me, I explained to students that in my mind, teacher-selected literature meant sustained silent reading, which meant that the literature component was reading of their choice, not mine.

I then designed assignments to cover each of the core curriculum writing requirements and spread them throughout the semester. I then figured how many news, feature, sports, editorial, and review articles each student could write with the time remaining and made a semester checklist based on both core writing and journalistic writing assignments.

From earlier experiences in teaching journalism, I realized that if we have a staff meeting on Monday and every student signs up for an article, we have started the process, but from there, anything can happen. For example, one student may take his topic, leave class, find his subject at lunch, get the interview, write the article that evening, and have it on the Web server by Tuesday morning. A second student may ask for an interview but find out that her subject is out of school for three days, so she has to wait until Thursday to get the interview and then write the article on Friday.

While both of these students begin class each day with SSR, the problem comes when we move to the writing portion of class. The first student finished his article on Tuesday. It isn't due until Friday, so now he does his SSR, then props his feet up on the desk (figuratively) and says, "I'm done for the week." The second student, panicked about not being able to get her interview until Thursday, but unable to work, says, "I can't do anything until I get that interview." Both have significant amounts of time that will be open, even though they are both doing their jobs.

While they represent the extremes of this time problem, almost every other student will encounter a time during the week when all computers are taken, the interview won't be done until after class, they left their interview notes at home, or thousands of other problems that stifle or stop production. I wanted a project, like SSR, that couldn't be finished ("I finished reading my book." "Good job. Bring a new one tomorrow.") but gave students the freedom of choice and control they thrive on in silent reading. I want it to be an ongoing, independent project any time their regular writing assignments were stalled or finished. I also wanted it to be a project that lasted throughout the entire school year. I decided to call it "the masterpiece."

As with SSR, students working on the masterpiece are free to choose the topic, length, genre, and style of writing they produce. Like many experiments, the first semester posed a few problems. The freedom of the assignment was exciting to the students, but some of them took the freedom beyond limits. Some turned in poster collages with a few words written around the edge or a book of photographs in which the only writing was the captions. One student turned in a videotape of him skiing and said, "That's the story I have to tell."

While I always appreciate creativity, those weren't really what I had in mind when I envisioned the masterpiece.

Other students who heard the same assignment in class turned in 35 pages containing four chapters of a novel (to be continued, of course), or 43 pages of a play script, complete with stage directions. They saved me. The masterpiece idea felt as right as SSR, and I wanted it to work. I had to rewrite the instructions, so I went directly to the best source for advice on these matters—my students. When I explained what my concerns were, most students were surprised by the collages and videotape. They knew that wasn't in the spirit of the assignment and were willing to help me with ideas. We brainstormed how to refine the guidelines. The next week, at the beginning of second semester, I handed out a much clearer (though more restrictive) set of guidelines. We discussed them one by one and at the end of class, I asked if there were any questions or concerns. No one spoke, until finally a senior girl said, "This will make it much easier." No one objected to anything. Based on their suggestions, the guidelines I'm currently using for the masterpiece appear in Figure 7.1.

These guidelines changed everything. In the masterpieces for second semester, the writing was varied, quality work, and it was a joy to read. The biggest difference was on the faces of the students when they turned in their projects, proud of what they had written. They had spent time on their projects and had become attached to what they were doing. It solved my time problem in journalism class as well, and when I surveyed students at the end of the year, their feedback was overwhelmingly positive. One senior boy, who wrote more than 60 pages on his masterpiece, commented, "The Masterpiece is your masterpiece."

While I love the concept of the masterpiece, I don't have the program completely in place yet. One of the reasons SSR works so well is that all students are quiet and reading; peer pressure helps focus the reading process. Writing workshop, on the other hand, is messy. Described accurately by Nancie Atwell in her book *In the Middle,* writers' workshop is full of activity, energy, movement, and

Figure 7.1

Masterpiece Guidelines

The masterpiece is an extended work of writing in which you choose the topic, writing style, genre, intended audience, and purpose. We will schedule work sessions in class for the masterpiece, but the bulk of the work on this will be on your own during the days when you cannot get to an interview subject or you finish another written assignment early. There are no free days in this class. If you have no other specific work to do for *Bronc Express,* you automatically know that your assignment that day is to work on your masterpiece. The guidelines for this assignment are:

1. This is an *extended writing assignment* and must be written specifically for this class. Do not turn in work credited to another class. Do not turn in diaries, scrapbooks, collages, posters, illustrations, videos, or photos as part of the project. A single photo or graphic may accompany the project, but it will not be graded and the time to produce it will not be considered in the calculation of the grade.

2. The content of the masterpieces follows the same rules as *Bronc Express* articles. Since drugs, alcohol, sex, violence, and profanity are not permitted at school, they are not permitted in masterpiece works.

3. The masterpiece should be fiction (long short story or short novel), nonfiction (biographical, autobiographical, historical, research, personal experience, etc.), a poetry collection, or a play script. Keep in mind that the final goal of this project (and of this class) is to publish, so be clear in your mind who your audience is and where you will be able to submit it (including *Bronc Express Online*).

4. The ultimate goal of this project is to work on a large project of your choosing over an extended period of time (like a professional writer), perfecting it into a work that you are proud of and are anxious to share with others.

5. We will have one read-around near the middle of each six-week period. You will need to read at least three pages of new writing at each read-around.

6. One week before the end of each six-week period, you will hand in a typed (12 point Times/Helvetica, double-spaced) publishable-quality manuscript (get help from editors, staff members, and/or adviser to correct errors) of eight or more pages.

7. This should be the very best work you can produce and will be graded as such.

quite often, noise. Students need to move, to go from computer to printer, to trade papers to edit, to talk about ideas. Valuable and necessary parts of the writing process, they also make it much easier for a student to slip away from the task at hand. During SSR, I am sitting silently, reading with them. During writing time, I am generally modeling writing by offering examples, suggesting words, reviewing interview questions, or solving computer problems. I'm engaged with them in writers' work, which makes it much easier for a student across the room to be off-task.

Having the masterpiece solves the problem of filling gaps in time with short, unconnected assignments or leaving students to fill the time on their own. In the same way that I worked to improve my SSR program over the years, I'll continue to experiment with the masterpiece, allowing it to evolve as needed. Although it was initially designed for newspaper class, I believe it could be modified to fit any level English class.

Because the newspaper class is specifically designed to publish student writing, it is easy to encourage students to publish everything they write for class. News, features, and sports articles are published in the school newspaper. Their core English assignments, however, wouldn't work well in the school paper. First, we couldn't afford to publish a paper large enough to accommodate that much writing, and more important, no one would want to read it. To establish a venue for the extra work, we created *Bronc Express Online,* a Web site modeled after professional newspapers and stored on our school's Web server (you can visit the site at http://senior.billings.k12.mt.us/bexpress).

A colleague of mine, Vince Long, who teaches computers, liked the idea of this project and assigned it to three of his advanced computer students. They took to the challenge and designed an excellent Web site that could easily house the various types of writings we would produce. They even went so far as to set up an online system to allow us to submit and edit our articles from our classroom. After they spent a semester setting up the program, we ran the show on our own with occasional technical help from Vince and his students. Because the server's memory is large, we have access to unlimited space and can publish everything we write, including the lengthy masterpiece writings.

Most English classes don't publish a school newspaper, but that doesn't mean students can't publish their work. The thrill of publication will take them a long way toward caring about what they write and will help them see the connection between reading and writing more clearly. Every semester I find opportunities for my English classes to submit poems or short stories to student literary magazines and contests. Here again, the Internet may be an excellent resource.

I found one Web opportunity for sophomore students through PBS's Masterpiece Theatre. They opened a literary site and wanted students to write biographies about writers from their home states. My students researched Montana writers, and we published 42 biographies on the literary map. The students thought this was a great assignment. In fact, several students became interested in the authors researched and later chose to read their books for SSR. Though this was a one-time project, similar opportunities exist if teachers keep their eyes open.

Another alternative is to create opportunities. *Bronc Express Online* was a good solution to our problem. Any English class could produce its own online newspaper or literary magazine using simple graphics and layout. Any high school has students who would love to design a Web site, and this type of publication offers several advantages. First, it is free, a major concern given the price of most print publishing in today's market. Second, space is generally unlimited. Text takes up very little space on a server, so even a moderately sized server holds thousands of pages of student writings. Third, it is instantaneous. Students can write and edit a poem today and see it online tomorrow. A print version of a literary magazine, while nice to look at and hold, may take months to finish, testing the patience of teachers and students alike.

My newspaper class is designed to get students' work published, so students who sign up for it expect to write publishable-quality articles regularly. In fact, I tell them, "You can't get a C in this class, because we can't publish C articles in our newspaper. You have to keep rewriting until you achieve an A." That approach works fine in this class but would not work for regular English classes, where writing for publication might happen a few times a year on a voluntary basis. I might explain the publication and what its editors are looking for, set a deadline, and collect work from the students who choose to participate. I might assign a few projects, like the Masterpiece Theatre literary biographies, for everyone. The degree of emphasis on publication can be adjusted to suit any class, but not having publication opportunities available to student writers seems, to me, like having my cross-country runners practice every day but never run a race. Attempting to publish articles will make students feel like real writers, and most often, they improve their writing accordingly. My goal with SSR is to have students become Good Adult Readers. My goal with writing is for students to make choices, experience challenges, and feel successes that arise from caring about and working seriously on significant pieces of writing. SSR forms the foundation, creating meaningful opportunities to share or publish writing, and filling out the language arts package.

8

Starting Your Own Program

Every summer, empty lots and small fields across the United States are filled with boys and girls learning to play T-ball. A parent places the ball on the tee, and the batter gets to do exactly what he wants to do—hit the ball and run. No striking out. No waiting for a pitcher who can't get the ball across the plate. No score. No loser.

Later on, when the children have grown, they can learn to hit a moving pitch, to throw a curve or slider, to steal second base. But first, they need to love the motion of hitting and running, of fielding and throwing, or they will never be interested in the more intricate aspects of the game of baseball.

Although the analogy is not identical, I suppose much of what I've been saying about SSR is like T-ball. SSR teaches basic skills and, as Krashen (1993) says, sets the foundation so that advanced language skills can follow. While T-ball players must wait until they move to the next league to try more advanced skills, SSR students often soar on their own, taking their reading and language skills to levels that neither they nor their teachers would have predicted. However, setting the foundation and instilling the joy of reading are what make SSR a powerful, successful tool. Without the foundation of reading for enjoyment, many students are unlikely to reach advanced levels of proficiency in the language arts.

SSR becomes especially significant in the face of today's high-pressure, high-stakes mandated testing. If teachers allow these tests to dictate curriculum content and withhold SSR as a result, they remove the fastest, most efficient means of helping students discover the pleasure of reading and deprive students of the most important attribute of a good education. If students learn that reading is only done so that they can pass a test, they will never become lifelong readers. Unfortunately, while many teachers say making lifelong learners is the goal of their program, they limit reading experiences to those that will improve test performance. Their actions speak a different language to their students.

Testing is not going to disappear, so we need to teach students the skills needed to meet those exams. SSR cost-effectively and efficiently teaches skills as well as enjoyment. If teachers clearly explain the SSR program and the benefits, students move easily in that direction and achieve the desired results.

Any teacher or parent who has read this far has obviously found something interesting about the idea of SSR and is, perhaps, considering using it in a classroom or home. That's great. Get started. Dig in. Find your own way. Explain the idea to your students tomorrow and begin reading the next day. Don't wait until the beginning of the next grading period. SSR doesn't need neat, organized time periods. It just needs time. Give the students time to read, and good things will happen.

Any teacher or parent who uses SSR for one year, a semester, or in some cases, a month will see positive and worthwhile things happening with students. In Chapter 6, I recounted some of the available research regarding SSR. After using SSR in the classroom, you will find, as I have, that the most important research about SSR walks into your room everyday. Over and over, students' actions and comments you see and hear will confirm the value of silent reading.

I often hear teachers say something like "I want to start SSR, but I can't convince other teachers to join me." Start by yourself then. I began on my own and experimented frequently until I found the right combination to make my program work. I've shared these ideas in this book. Use them to help you, or try your own variations to see how it works. SSR is more of a guideline than a structured program, and teachers, as well as classes of students, have personalities that make some approaches more effective. Be open to trying new things, and by all means, listen to what the students are saying.

Getting several teachers to start at the same time might be helpful, but it could also create problems. If you have all discussed SSR and agreed on similar guidelines, it should work well. If you can't agree, or if others are hesitant, start alone. I never try to convince a teacher to use SSR, but when they walk by my classroom, day after day, and see my students quietly reading, many ask questions about what I'm doing and how I get kids to participate so well. Then I'll explain the program, but it is still their choice, because it changes the dynamics of the classroom: students read independently and assume control of an important part of their education. Coercing any teacher to start SSR, either through peer pressure or mandated staff development, will not work. The resentment will undermine the SSR process. Better to start SSR without them and let them see how much fun you are having.

When I've talked to teachers who are hesitant or clearly against using SSR in the classroom, I have found some of their objections to be interesting. The first concern, which we dealt with earlier, is the time conflict with the core curriculum.

Another concern is with the silence itself. Some see that silence as boring, perhaps even frightening, as if nothing important could happen unless accompanied by noise. I love the silence. It is a wonderful respite from much of the rest of the day, and many of my students (see their comments in Chapter 5) feel the same way. I'm reminded of the comment of the Norwegian explorer Nansen after he returned from three years in the high Arctic in the 1890s. "Silent, oh, so silent! You can hear the vibrations of your own nerves," he wrote (1999, p. 228). It is good, I expect, for all of us to hear our own nerves vibrate at times.

Teachers may also hesitate to give students so much control. In SSR, students get to choose what books they read, when to quit a book, when to start a new book, when to read two books at the same time, when to reread a book they have read before, when to change genres, and when to let great ideas come into their heads. As a witness of this process for over two decades, I know that they are capable of making those choices. In fact, *capable* is a mild word to describe it. Most of them thrive on making those choices, and any concern with students taking that kind of control is an issue that teachers have to get past in order to let SSR run its course in the classroom.

Students frequently complain that schoolwork is not relevant to their lives. "When will we ever use this?" they ask. But with SSR, because they choose their own books, they never make that complaint. It is extremely relevant and is kept so with each succeeding book choice. Their interests drive each book selection. Their curiosities direct them to each new topic or genre.

Teachers or parents who start SSR programs should keep things simple. It is a reading program. Let the students read. The teacher needs to provide the opportunity, then get out of the way. Time is the first thing students need. They also need the modeling of an adult reader, and they may need some guidance from time to time, but mostly they need the confirmation from an adult that they are capable of becoming good readers. One pleasant surprise for both students and teachers is that students often discover that they are far better readers than they could ever have believed. Let them begin reading, and watch the drama unfold.

Few students want to fail, to read poorly, or to get bad grades. They want to succeed and be good students, but time, energy, and conflicts get in their way and they give up. SSR gives time and place, putting everyone in the room into the mode of reading, enjoying, and sharing books. In an SSR classroom, it's okay to like a book and say so.

Many students get so interested in books they won't quit. Other teachers have come to me to complain that my students won't stop reading in their classrooms. They become good at hiding books under the table or inside their textbooks in order to sneak in a few more minutes.

When they reach this stage, students often ask for more reading time. Students who finish a quiz or assignment early may have extra reading time, the reward I give for efficient work, for working ahead, or for being a good student. I don't give extra credit, only extra reading time.

Because I firmly believe that education is an ongoing, continuous, self-selected process, it has been easy for me to stick with SSR. I've seen hundreds of fads come and go and seen theories change and cycle back on themselves. SSR has been the one program that has been a thread running through a quarter century of teaching. I realize now that I could never plan to teach all the learning that happens during SSR. I just remind myself of the success stories I've seen and that sometimes it takes one book to change a reader's life.

A few years ago, I had a student who talked frequently during SSR. It wasn't loud, but silent reading is silent. I stopped her several times, then moved her across the room so she couldn't talk to anyone. Upset, she met with her counselor, who happens to be a fan of SSR. When she came to class the next day, she asked to talk to me in the hall. She apologized for her interruptions and said, "I guess I just didn't understand how sacred the silent reading time was."

References

Aranha, M. (1985). Sustained silent reading goes east. *The Reading Teacher, 39*(2), 214–217.

Arthur, J. (1995). *What is the effect of recreational reading on reading achievement of middle grade students?* (ERIC Document Reproduction Service No. ED 391 143)

Atwell, N. (1987). *In the middle: Writing, reading, and learning with adolescents.* Upper Montclair, NJ: Boynton/Cook.

Block, C., & Mangieri, J. (2002). Recreational reading: 20 years later. *The Reading Teacher, 55*(6), 572–580.

Chow, P., & Chou, C. (2000). Evaluating sustained silent reading in reading classes [Online article]. *The Internet TESL Journal, VI*(11). Available: http://iteslj.org/Articles/Chow-SSR.html

Csikszentmihalyi, M. (1991). *Flow: The psychology of optimal experience.* New York: Harper Perennial.

Csikszentmihalyi, M. (1996). *Creativity: Flow and the psychology of discovery and invention.* New York: HarperCollins.

Cullinan, B. (2000). *Independent reading and school achievement* [Online article]. Available: http://www.ala.org/aasl/SLMR/vol3/independent/independent

Dwyer, E., & West, R. (1994). *Effects of sustained silent reading on reading rate among college students.* (ERIC Document Reproduction Service No. ED 382 924)

Ellis, N. (1995). Vocabulary acquisition: Psychological perspectives. *The Language Teacher, 19*(2), 12–16.

Flannery, M. (2004). Cybercheating. *NEA Today, 23*(3), 40–42.

Gardiner, S. (2001a). Cybercheating: A new twist on an old problem. *Phi Delta Kappan, 83*(2), 172–174.

Gardiner, S. (2001b). Ten minutes a day for silent reading. *Educational Leadership, 59*(2), 32–35.

Gardner, H. (1991). *The unschooled mind: How children think and how schools should teach.* New York: Basic Books.

Hunt, L. (1997). The effect of self-selection, interest, and motivation upon independent, instructional and frustrational levels. *Reading Teacher, 50*(4), 278–282.

Kornelly, D., & Smith, L. (1993). Bring back the USSR. *School Library Journal, 39*(4), 48.

Krashen, S. (1993). *The power of reading: Insights from the research.* Englewood, CO: Libraries Unlimited.

Krashen, S. (2001). More smoke and mirrors: A critique of the National Reading Panel report on fluency. *Phi Delta Kappan, 83*(2), 119–132.

Krashen, S. (2003). False claims about phonemic awareness, phonics, skills vs. whole language, and recreational reading [Online article]. NoChildLeft.com. Available: http://nochildleft.com/2003/may03reading.html

Marzano, R., Pickering, D., & Pollock, J. (2001). *Classroom instruction that works: Research-based strategies for increasing student achievement.* Alexandria, VA: Association for Supervision and Curriculum Development.

McCracken, R., & McCracken, M. (1978). Modeling is the key to sustained silent reading. *The Reading Teacher, 31*(4), 406–408.

McKenna, M., Kear, D., & Ellsworth, R. (1995). Children's attitudes toward reading: A national survey. *Reading Research Quarterly, 30*(4), 934–956.

Melton, E. (1993). *SSR: Is it an effective practice for the learning disabled?* (ERIC Document Reproduction Service No. ED 397 569)

Murray, D. (1987). *Write to learn.* New York: Holt, Rinehart and Winston.

Nagy, W., & Anderson, R. (1984). How many words are there in printed school English? *Reading Research Quarterly, 19*(3), 304–328.

Nagy, W., Anderson, R., & Herman, P. (1987). Learning word meanings from context during normal reading. *American Educational Research Journal, 24*(2), 237–270.

Nansen, F. (1999). *Farthest north.* London: Random House.

National Reading Panel (2000). *Report of the National Reading Panel: Teaching children to read.* Available: http://www.nichd.nih.gov/publications/nrp/findings.htm

Nell, V. (1988). The psychology of reading for pleasure: Needs and gratifications. *Reading Research Quarterly, 23*(1), 7–20.

Pilgreen, J. (2000). *The SSR handbook: How to organize and manage a sustained silent reading program.* Portsmouth, NH: Boynton/Cook.

Pyle, V. (1990). SSRW—beyond silent reading. *Journal of Reading, 33*(5), 379–380.

Saragi, Y., Nation, P., & Meister, G. (1978). Vocabulary learning and reading. *System, 6,* 70–78.

Scherer, M. (2004). What works in reading? *Educational Leadership, 61*(6), 5.

Tipaldi, E. (2004). Squeezing reading into our students' lives [Online article]. *Western Massachusetts Writing Project.* Available: http://www.umass.edu/wmwp/programs/Research99/tipaldi.htm

Tovani, C. (2000). *I read it, but I don't get it: Comprehension strategies for adolescent readers.* Portland, ME: Stenhouse Publishers.

Trelease, J. (2001). *The read-aloud handbook.* New York: Penguin Books.

U.S. Department of Education. Institute of Education Sciences. National Center for Education Statistics. (2003). *The Nation's Report Card: Reading 2002.* NCES 2003-521. Washington, DC.

U.S. Department of Education. Institute of Education Sciences. National Center for Education Statistics. (2003). *The Nation's Report Card: Writing 2002.* NCES 2003-529. Washington, DC.

U.S. Department of Education. Office of the Secretary. Office of Public Affairs. (2003). *No child left behind: A parents guide.* Available: http://www.ed.gov/parents/academic/involve/nclbguide/parentsguide.pdf

Valeri-Gold, M. (1995). Uninterrupted sustained silent reading is an effective authentic method for college developmental learners. *Journal of Reading, 38*(5), 385–386.

Von Sprecken, D., Kim, J., & Krashen, S. (2000). The home run book: Can one positive reading experience create a reader? *California School Library Journal, 23*(2), 8–9.

Weller, L., & Weller, S. (1999). Secondary school reading: Using the quality principle of continuous improvement to build an exemplary program. *NASSP Bulletin, 83*(607), 59–68.

Further Reading

Culham, R. (2003). *6 + 1 traits of writing: The complete guide (grades 3 and up)*. New York: Scholastic Professional Books.

Fisher, D. (2001). We're moving on up: Creating a schoolwide literacy effort in an urban high school. *Journal of Adolescent & Adult Literacy, 45*(2), 92–100.

Gallagher, K. (2003). *Reading reasons: Motivational mini-lessons for middle and high school*. Portland, ME: Stenhouse Publishers.

Gauthier, M., & Smith, E. (1993). Whole school supplemental reading program. *Journal of Reading, 37*(2), 135–137.

Hopkins, G. (1997). 'Sustained silent reading' helps develop independent readers (and writers) [Online article]. *Education World*. Available: http://www.educationworld.com/a_curr/curr038.shtml

Marson, W. (2002). Free voluntary reading (FVR) pays big dividends [Online article]. *Education World*. Available: http://www.educationworld.com/a_curr/curr007.shtml

Meyers, R. (1998). *Uninterrupted sustained silent reading*. Long Beach, CA: California State University. (ERIC Document Reproduction No. ED 418 379)

Ohanian, S. (1997). Some are more equal than others. *Phi Delta Kappan, 78*(6), 471–475.

Robertson, C., Keating, I., Shenton, L., & Roberts, I. (1996). Uninterrupted, sustained, silent reading: The rhetoric and the practice. *Journal of Research in Reading, 19*(1), 25–35.

Speaker, R. (1990). Another twist on sustained silent reading: SSR + D. *Journal of Reading, 34*(2), 143–144.

Index

Note: An *f* after a page number indicates a figure.

About the Author

Steve Gardiner, an English and journalism teacher at Billings Senior High School in Billings, Montana, has used sustained silent reading in his classroom for 27 years. He is a National Board Certified Teacher and also is certified as a Master Journalism Educator by the Journalism Education Association. He has published more than 500 articles in newspapers and magazines and has written three books about mountain climbing. Gardiner has climbed mountains in Greenland, Alaska, Europe, South America, Africa, and Asia, and recently ran the Boston Marathon. Visit Gardiner's Web site at www.readandrun.com.

Related ASCD Resources

At the time of publication, the following ASCD resources were available; for the most up-to-date information about ASCD resources, go to www.ascd.org. ASCD stock numbers are noted in parentheses.

Networks

Visit the ASCD Web site (www.ascd.org) and search for "networks" for information about professional educators who have formed groups around topics like "Language, Literacy, and Literature." Look in the "Network Directory" for current facilitators' addresses and phone numbers.

Mixed Media

Literacy Across the Curriculum Professional Development Planner and Resource Package (#703400)

Reading Strategies for the Content Areas, volumes 1 and 2 (ASCD Action Tool) by Sue Beers and Lou Howell (Volume 1: #703109; Volume 2: #705002)

Print Products

ASCD Topic Pack: Reading (#198215 print and electronic versions)

Educational Leadership: What Research Says About Reading (entire issue, March 2004) and *Reading and Writing in the Content Areas* (entire issue, November 2002). Excerpted articles online free; entire issue online and accessible to ASCD members.

Literacy Leadership for Grades 5–12 by Rosemary Taylor and Valerie Doyle Collins (#103022)

Literacy Strategies for Grades 4–12: Reinforcing the Threads of Reading by Karen Tankersley (#104428)

The Multiple Intelligences of Reading and Writing: Making the Words Come Alive by Thomas Armstrong (#102280)

Research-Based Methods of Reading Instruction, Grades K–3 by Sharon Vaughn and Sylvia Linan-Thompson (#104134)

Teaching Reading in the Content Areas: If Not Me, Then Who? 2nd Edition by Rachel Billmeyer and Mary Lee Barton (#397258)

Using Data to Assess Your Reading Program by Emily Calhoun (book with CD-ROM) (#102268)

Video

The Lesson Collection: Literacy Strategies (Tapes 49–56) (#405160 VHS)

The Lesson Collection: Reading Strategies (Tapes 1–8) (#499257 VHS)

The Lesson Collection: Reading Strategies 2 (Tapes 25–32) (#402034 VHS)

The Multiple Intelligences of Reading and Writing: Making the Words Come Alive Books-in-Action (#403325 VHS)

Reading in the Content Areas Video Series (3 videotapes) (#402029)

For more information, visit us on the World Wide Web (http://www.ascd.org), send an e-mail message to member@ascd.org, call the ASCD Service Center (1-800-933-ASCD or 703-578-9600, then press 2), send a fax to 703-575-5400, or write to Information Services, ASCD, 1703 N. Beauregard St., Alexandria, VA 22311-1714 USA.